MIND SIGHT
Learning Through Imaging

Beverly-Colleene Galyean

Published By

Center for Integrative Learning

1442-A Walnut St., Ste. 317
Berkeley, CA 94709

ABOUT THE

CENTER FOR INTEGRATIVE LEARNING

We are witnessing a growing interest in human development, consciousness, human potential and mind power. Futurists tell us that the emerging mind skills of today will be the basics of tomorrow. The **CENTER FOR INTEGRATIVE LEARNING** was founded to meet the needs of people whose inner visions have led them to seek out integrative, holistic means for exploring and expanding their own capabilities, for releasing untapped personal potential, and for teaching these processes to others.

In the past we concentrated much of our energy on traditional education systems where we gave numerous workshops, seminars and training sessions to individual faculties, school districts, colleges and universities, and private education centers as well. **Mind Sight** is the "crown jewel," the culmination of our work in education over the years.

Our work has taught us much. We learned that the Mind Sight processes we taught educators, counselors, therapists, parents and students are also powerful tools to use for bodily healing, accelerated thinking, opening up intuitive insight, and training intuitive intelligence.

Many who come to us are faced with life threatening diseases, or emotional crises, or are in the midst of challenging life transitions. Others come to open up and expand their intelligence to include mastery of the intuitive and metaphoric ways of knowing that are considered to be the most important mind skills of the future. Our graduate degree program (a joint venture with International College of Los Angeles) in Transpersonal Psychology and Consciousness Studies enables those interested in scholarly studies to pursue theoretical as well as experiential research on the themes we have targeted in our work.

The Center offers personal counseling, ongoing therapeutic work, weekly support groups, monthly seminars, dream workshops and annual retreats as well as graduate studies. Our primary interest, our farthest reaching vision and most permeating dream is to help all of us "come to know the miracle we are."

For information concerning our programs and publications write to:
Center for Integrative Learning
1442-A Walnut St., Ste. 317
Berkeley, CA 94709

Cover Design: Patti Wallace
Photographs: Anne Bruetsch
           Beverly-Colleene Galyean
Editing/Layout: Anne Bruetsch

First Printing: 1983
Second Printing: 1986
Third Printing: 1988

SPECIAL THANKS

Thank you, Anne, for urging me to write this book, and for the countless hours you've spent organizing the material into a suitable format. You've been my guide, typist, editor, photographer and graphics specialist. Through the beauty and love of your imaging "I", you've brought <u>Mind Sight</u> out of the depths of my imaging "Me" and made it possible for everyone who reads our book to share in the wonderful work we've done with imagery these past years.

To all of you, my dear friends, who've been using imagery in your own personal and professional lives, my deepest gratitude. Together we are creating learning activities that are opening up our minds and expanding our potentials beyond our wildest dreams.

And to those of you who have worked with us over the years and have contributed to our research your own personal insights as well as samples of imagery work done in your own education settings, my heartfelt thanks. Because of you and your energies on behalf of imagery work, we are growing every day in understanding the vast physical, emotional, intellectual and spiritual potentials that are opening up for us to understand and use for the betterment of the entire planet.

FOREWORD

We believe that "mind sight" is one of our greatest gifts as human beings. Since the beginning of time, our ancestors and now ourselves have grown in knowledge, wisdom and creative insight through illuminative inner experiences. All discoveries, scientific findings and creative inventions start with a clear inner vision of what could be. And once these visions, called "ideas" resonate strongly enough within us, we find the means with which to birth them in everyday life.

The cover of <u>Mind Sight</u> depicts our favorite symbols, symbols that have emerged within the consciousness of many people working with us. They represent our most cherished dreams for ourselves and the world in which we live. The rose is our love, love that creates new life and new possibilities from the heart where ultimate good is willed toward everyone and everything in the universe. The butterfly is us, free to be born again and again through the frequent death experiences that greet us throughout life. With each experience, our passion for life and the wonders inherent in life grows stronger and stronger. The castle is inner wisdom, the source of knowing that directs us to make excellent decisions about our lives. It is the place we go to answer the questions we ourselves have posed.

The face is androgynous, representing perfect harmony between the creative-receptive energies of the female, and the creative-active energies of the male. It is androgyny that hands us exquisite dreams of joy and well-being as natural conditions of life, and it is androgyny that enables us to actualize these dreams in everyday life.

The entire "mind sight" process takes place within the fertile darkness of our own consciousness. We enter the quiet peace within us, the place of knowing that lies deep within each human being, and call forth those images, visions, dreams and subsequent feelings that communicate ever fresh information on human potential, life on this planet, extraterrestrial life, and cosmic aspects of the universe. Our inner visions are the fabric of creative thought, the herald of possible realities, the womb where that which could be becomes that which is.

We approach <u>Mind Sight</u> with reverence, a reverence that honors the unique manner in which everyone whom we've met has told of their imagery experiences, and has shared their very best dreams about themselves and their world. As we listen to these narratives around the fires of our education settings, counseling centers and homes, we realize that they are providing us with magnificent blueprints for a world that has already come - a world founded upon love, trust, open communication and shared resources. A world such as this can only know peace!

*I can give you nothing
that has not already its
being within yourself.
I can throw open to you
no picture gallery but
your own . . . I help you
to make your own world
visible. That is all.*

H. Hesse

CONTENTS

CHAPTER EIGHT: GUIDED AFFECTIVE IMAGERIES 199

CHAPTER NINE: GUIDED TRANSPERSONAL IMAGERIES . 281

INTRODUCTION

Remember a wonderful day in your life? This was a day when everything seemed so beautiful. It was an extra special day, a day that was made just for you. Who was there with you - if anyone? What was happening? What made this day so special?

Now remember a time when you laughed so hard you almost cried. Or maybe you did cry from laughing so hard. What was going on? Who was there with you, if anyone?

Now remember a time when you were terribly nervous. Perhaps your knees were knocking, your stomach tied up in one huge knot, your hands icy cold and/or rather clammy. You could hardly breathe and your mouth was desert dry. What was happening at that time to make you so nervous?

What does your immune system look like when fighting germs?

Now think about the future, one thousand years into the future. Describe what cities will look like, transportation, people, food, money.

In order to do these exercises, you had to create pictures in your mind. Some pictures were of past events, whereas others were of future possibilities. Certain feelings accompanied these pictures, feelings such as peace, joy, excitement, satisfaction, fear, nervousness and caution. Did you notice that, regardless of whether your pictures were of the past or future, your feelings were in the present moment? In fact, your images were also in the present moment and you experienced them as present phenomena to be felt in your "here and now" moment of conscious awareness. Right now as you are reading these words, thousands of images accompanied by feeling tones are passing through your mind. Your mind is translating these words into images and vibrations so that your brain can process and make sense out of the information coming into you.

The term "thinking" is synonymous with "seeing and feeling the pictures in our mind". Sometimes individual pictures give us information. At other times we must watch short or lengthy "films" being produced in our minds before we can receive any coherent message. The stronger the emotional impact (imprint) of these vibratory images, the more we remember of the picture and the more we learn. Thus the ability to learn more, and to learn more quickly such as geniuses do, corresponds to how well we can work with our sensing, feeling, imaging mind.

As you begin your work with visualization and guided imagery, expect (see and feel yourself having) wonderful results. Focus deeply on the pictures within yourself, the images floating softly through your inner screen that tell you how your own mind is understanding whatever information is presented to it. You will begin to clearly see what it is that you know, and what it is that you are about to learn. Your realm of possible realities (those things that could be) will expand tremendously. This is how the genius mind works. And it is this genius mind we are nurturing through the Mind Sight imagery processes.

In Mind Sight, we share with you our expertise, thousands of hours of designing, refining and evaluating visualization and guided imagery work. Our journey in this regard has been and continues to be joyful beyond words. You bring to Mind Sight the power of your imaging mind and Mind Sight brings to you the processes necessary for mining the wealth of this imaging mind, the parent of genius, the initiator of great discovery, the guide for all science, the mentor of self-knowledge and acceptance, and the sage revealing universal and cosmic knowledge to humankind. It is now up to you and those working with you to give these imageries your fully focused and loving attention, and to watch the imageries perform their wonders through and for you and all of us.

Mind Sight holds the full tapestry of our learnings over the years. Along the way we have met many people representative of numerous personal, cultural, socio-political and religious values and belief systems, and we have honored all of these in our work. We have found that some people consider imagery as a primary means for relaxing and reducing stress, focusing attention and quieting mind chatter. These imageries are included in the chapter titled Getting Started. Many people with whom we have worked are primarily concerned with cognitive achievement and academic gains. These imageries are found in the Guided Cognitive Imagery chapter.

Others value imagery for its ability to lead us to self-learning and greater inner awareness of feelings, personal needs and wants, self-concept and esteem, deeper bondings and increased interpersonal skills with others. These imageries are included in the Guided Affective Imagery chapter. There are also those whose interests lie in the areas of futuristics, expanded mind skills, exploration of human potential and the study of metaphysical, cosmic and spiritual themes. These imageries are found in the Guided Transpersonal Imagery chapter.

Mind Sight not only reflects a wide diversity of preferences regarding imagery work, but it was written to serve the needs of all people wishing to use visualization and guided imagery in their lives. We suggest that those of you using our materials, first identify the needs and preferences of those working with you (i.e., community, parents, students, peers, clients, etc.), and then select your imageries accordingly.

As you begin (or continue) your work with imagery, know that you share in the expertise and loving thoughts of thousands of others who have discovered what miracles of learning, understanding and love come about when we call upon our imaging mind to communicate knowledge to us.

CHAPTER ONE

THE IMAGING MIND

IMAGERY, CONSCIOUSNESS AND INTELLIGENCE

While exploring the dynamics of consciousness and the evolution of intelligence, we discover again and again what has always been known intuitively: that thinking is a moving projection of vibratory images that appear within the mind and are felt throughout the body. The fact that we are "conscious" means that we are able to see and learn from the imagery vignettes passing through our minds. As humans, we are essentially "image forming" beings whose ability to discover, understand and create new meanings and communicate depends largely on our ability to form and recognize the significance of inner images and their accompanying sensations and feeling tones.

Imagery has always played a central part in intellectual endeavors. For example, when we look at how geniuses think, how they have described their own intellectual capabilities, it is clear that they are highly sensitive to their own mental pictures and to the feelings and sensations that accompany these images. By his own admission, we know that Einstein's ability to resolve complex physical/mathematical problems was accomplished by his keen ability to perceive and work with inner images. Words, ideas and logical resolutions came later.

> "The interaction of images is the source of thought. The words of the language as they are written or spoken do not seem to play any role in my mechanism of thought. The physical entities which seem to serve as elements of thought are ... clear images which can be voluntarily reproduced or combined." (Einstein in Ghiselin, 1952.)

The interplay of images seemed to be the essential factor in his productive thought.

Similar statements have issued from other creative geniuses. Aristotle believed that thought itself consisted of images, and that these images were empowered to evoke emotions that revealed inner knowing or knowledge. Pythagoras taught his disciples to seek solutions to complex mathematical problems in dream imagery. The German chemist Kekule discovered the molecular structure of benzene while receiving an image of a snake swallowing its tail. The French mathematician Poincare solved mathematical problems in moments of creative reverie. Leonardo da Vinci visualized the steam engine and the helicopter centuries before either were invented.

IMAGERY: PARENT OF SCIENCE AND TECHNOLOGY

The desire to harness the power of the imaging mind is as old as humanity. The ancients of all cultures filled their folkloric epics with tales of visions, dreams, intuitive insights and internal dialogues with higher beings or divinities whom they recognized as the sources of ultimate wisdom and knowledge. Early people believed that their dreams and fantasies were sent by the gods as blueprints for human creativity. Everything that has been invented by human endeavor started as an image "dream" or scenario of pictures in someone's mind (or in many people's minds). Imagery is the parent of technology.

Contemporary scientists also mention the importance of inner vision, intuition and imagination in scientific discovery. Capra (1975) describes how scientific research relies heavily on intuitive imaginative activity for clarifying and expanding rational operations.

> "The rational part of research would, in fact, be useless
> if it were not complimented by the intuition that gives
> scientists new insights and makes them creative..." (p. 31)

Scientific discoveries begin with an insightful inner vision of what could be. This vision is often referred to as a "hunch" that tantalizes the scientist's mind to verify its possibility through scientific investigation. When enough people admit to having the same "hunch" about possible reality, we see new forms or ideas materializing in the world around us. Many ancients dreamed about the sun as the

6

center of our universe before Copernicus ever demonstrated this to be true. Pluto was imagined in the minds of many astrologers before it was ever seen through a telescope. Countless physicians believed in the possibility of organ transplants before modern surgeons ever perfected the surgical procedure. Hans Berger knew that the brain emitted electrical waves years before he was able to invent the EEG machine to prove the existence of brain waves to his colleagues. Today's creative vision well may be tomorrow's great scientific discovery.

Because history has demonstrated the importance of the imaging mind in bettering human life, imagery work has evolved to become its own science. The terms "visualization" and "guided imagery" refer to the process whereby individuals are led on journeys into their imaging mind and respond to certain themes or suggestions by means of mental pictures. Someone (a leader or guide) suggests a theme such as "walking in a beautiful forest" or "talking to a wise counselor" and the imaging mind creates a situation that corresponds to this theme. Imagers observe their pictures, describe what they are seeing and feeling, and quietly allow the images to communicate insight or meaning to them. These insights and meanings may come immediately, or days, weeks, months, even years later.

IMAGERY IN PSYCHOLOGY AND MEDICINE

The use of guided imagery in psychology and medicine is spreading rapidly. Freud (Strachey, 1940), Jung (1964), Maslow (1954), DeSoille (1965), Leuner (1969), Shorr (1974) and Singer (1974) have pioneered using imagery techniques in psychology, counseling and psychotherapy. Initially used as a tool by Freud and his followers for uncovering various pathological drives within the human psyche, the trend changed significantly with Jung's work on the subconscious. Imagery became a "health" tool for uncovering through symbol and metaphoric language, basic human drives as well as cosmic/spiritual energies present throughout the universe as they impact human life.

Commencing with Maslow (1954) and continuing with the early humanists such as May (1961, 1968), Rogers (1961, 1980) and Bugenthal (1967), we note an interest in using imagery as a means for self-awareness, for charting aspects of human personality as these aspects reveal themselves in moments of introspection and meditation upon human life and human potential. Visions of "who we are" and "who we are coming to be" manifest strongly in their work with various growth groups engaging in introspective guided imagery types of activities. The recognition of inner strengths, sources of personal power, connections with the divine in all life, and deep bondedness with all others including the vegetable and mineral kingdoms becomes a central theme of much imagery work.

Following the work of these humanists, transpersonal psychologists and professionals such as Assagioli (1965), Schwarz (1978), Tart (1975), Walsh and Vaughan (1980) and Wilber (1977) extend these themes to include the study of expanded (beyond the ordinary rational cause-effect types of experiences) capabilities such as altered states, synergic mind, ESP, mind merging, cellular control and regeneration, out of body, psychokinetic, "peak" spiritual experiences, euphoric moments, spiritual visions, and healing abilities. Transpersonal imagery is often used to help individuals experience one or more of these phenomena such as transferring energy from one person to another for the purpose of bondedness or healing, or traveling into symbols of Higher Mind such as castles and mountains to receive insightful ideas about specific concerns.

Medical professionals are also turning to the use of imagery to assist in the healing process. Writing about holistic health practices, Jaffe (1980), Joy (1979), Oyle (1975), Pelletier (1977, 1978), Moss (1981) and Simonton (1978) indicate that imagery is currently being used to assist healing in all parts of the body. People are directed to: 1) Visualize themselves as healthy. 2) See tumors or other organismic disorders disappearing. 3) Empower medications and radiations to cooperate with and/or to accelerate the body's natural healing powers. 4) Image partially paralyzed limbs as fully functional. 5) Image failing eyesight as once again perfect. 6) Dialogue with physical disorders (symptoms), asking them to reveal their causes and reasons (things to be learned) to the person having them. 7) See healing energy (light) flooding the body and washing away all disease.

Imagery used in conjunction with biofeedback is becoming a familiar therapeutic intervention in preventative as well as curative medicine and psychology. By monitoring the degree of stress produced by the sometimes negative inner images we hold about ourselves and others, and the world "out there" as well, and by learning to change stressful images to healthy ones, individuals are able to control body

8

temperature, blood pressure, adrenalin and blood sugar levels, thereby alleviating stress responses in the body. They are also able to control various states of consciousness by regulating the vibratory rate of brain wave activity (Brown, 1977, 1980), Green and Green, 1977).

IMAGERY IN EDUCATION

Visualization, guided imagery and imagery-based curricular activities are also on the rise in many education programs. Influenced by successful endeavors in psychology and medicine, educators are becoming more attentive to curricular interventions that correspond to physical, emotional and spiritual well-being as well as intellectual growth. Interest in teaching to the intuitive, imaginative, metaphoric mind (often referred to as the "right brain") as well as to the rational, analytical mind (often called "left brain") is also growing. Intuitive activities such as fantasy, imagination, visualization, imagery and psychophysical exercises are becoming key aspects of standard curricula.

Imagery as used in education settings usually falls into one or more of four categories. (1) Relaxing, centering, focusing. These prepare the mind for learning by lessening stress, disinhibiting negative thoughts about learning, and sharpening inner vision. (2) Accelerating and expanding cognitive mastery. Students use imagery activities to increase their knowledge of cognitive material, basic subjects, technical skills and psychomotor skills. (3) Deepening affective growth and awareness of inner life. Students use affective imagery processes where they learn the skills of introspection, self-understanding, love and appreciation, bonding with others, empathy, communication, non-violent conflict resolution, problem solving, emotional assessment and self-determined self-concept. (4) Transpersonal growth. Students use imagery to explore aspects of consciousness that span beyond ordinary awakening states of perception such as transcendence, altered states, heightened sensory perception, and expanded intellectual capabilities (metaphoric thinking, symbolic language, mind merging or synergic mind, and direct mind to mind communication). They also explore spiritual themes such as "higher wisdom", "cosmic or universal consciousness", "oneness of being", "divine", and "universal love". When two or more of these types of imageries are merged into one lesson for the simultaneous teaching of different types of learning objectives (i.e., a cognitive objective merged

9

with an affective objective), we call this confluent imagery.

The following is an example of confluent imagery where objectives from all four domains are treated. The students begin with a "relaxing, centering, focusing activity" (readiness or preparing to learn), and then proceed with an imagery exercise to learn about "The Raven" (cognitive), explore their own inner sensations, feelings, images and thoughts by contacting a dream (affective), and dialogue with their inner wisdom (transpersonal).

A group of eleventh grade students is about to read "The Raven" by Poe. The room has been slightly darkened and a musical selection by Bach is playing softly in the background. The room offers a feeling of tranquility, mellowness and warmth. The teacher has added a bluish tone to the room by laying a sheet of blue cellophane across the overhead projector. In a quiet voice, the teacher announces that they will work with dreams during today's class, and that this experience relates to themes treated in "The Raven". The students respond with a feeling of focused expectation, knowing that something interesting and meaningful is about to happen. The teacher has them close their eyes, take three deep breaths, exhale any tiredness or distraction they are feeling, experience the peacefulness and quiet within themselves, and travel away to the world of dreams. Here they will find one special dream, a dream that will reveal an important message to them.

> "Let's begin our journey into the world of dreams by quieting our minds...On the count of three take a deep breath and fill your lungs with the fresh air around you...One...two...three...Take a deep breath, and let this feeling of lightness permeate every cell in your body... making you lighter and lighter...and brighter and brighter(pause)...Now exhale with a slight sigh and breathe out any tiredness or tension you may be feeling(pause). (Repeat deep breathing procedure two or more times until you sense that the students are relaxed)...Now gently float away from this room...Feel yourself moving through time and space to the land of dreams where one very special dream awaits you(pause)...Arrive at the land of dreams and look for one special dream to come and greet

10

dreams and look for one special dream to come and greet you...This dream belongs to you and wants to communicate an important message to you...If, by chance, no dream appears, then use this time to enjoy the peacefulness within you...This dream may appear to you at another time. If your dream does appear...ask it to give you an important message that will help you better understand yourself and what is going on in your life right now(pause)...If your dream tells you anything that doesn't seem to make sense to you...then ask it any questions that might help you better understand the message...You have one minute to meet and learn from your dream(pause)... Finish this dialogue with your dream and end by asking it to stay with you...to serve as the voice of your inner wisdom advising you how to make good helpful choices throughout your entire life(pause)... Now thank your dream for coming to speak with you and prepare yourself to return back here...fully alert and refreshed...and more knowledgeable about yourself and your life...Remember that anytime you feel you need advice you can always travel to your land of dreams and ask one special dream to talk with you... (pause)...On the count of three take a slow...deep breath...hold it...now exhale with a slight sigh and gently open your eyes...Wiggle your feet and hands...stretch your legs and arms..."

The students are then given crayons, markers and paper and asked to draw the experience in any way they wish. Following this meditative art activity, they talk with others about their experiences. They then write short accounts of their imagery journey, placing special emphasis on the dialogue and message received from their dream. In order to assure a free unblocked flow of information from the inner mind, the teacher has the students write their accounts in the first person narrative as if they were still in the imagery encountering the dream. The following is taken from a composition written by an eleventh grader:

11

In my dream I saw a high mountain with a castle on top. There was much sun shining on the castle giving it a silverish tone - sort of like magic. I am in a house at the bottom of the mountain. There is a road on my left leading to the castle. "Dream, speak to me!"

"Michelle, right now in your life you are searching for truth. My sun is the wisdom within you and is always available as your guide. The castle is your inner self which houses all truth. You must go there inside whenever you want to know what is right. Remember, you will always have a clear road to get you to your castle inside but you must make an effort to get there. My rainbow is my promise of great rewards for you. Don't ever be afraid. Sometimes there will be some clouds getting in your way but just keep on walking higher to your castle. The clouds will fly away."

The teacher directed the students to write their descriptions on these drawings and display them around the room for everyone to read. The students appeared to read them with an attitude of respect and appreciation for the unique experiences revealed by each person. They were deeply involved in the dream work, so much so that when "The Raven" was read in class, the students readily contrasted their inner experiences with those related by Poe. Terms such as "stream of consciousness", "symbolic expression", "metaphor" and "analog" became real for the students when they were presented the opportunity to live the themes within the unique workings of their own mind. Imagery enabled them to receive, process, recreate and express cognitive material in a manner congruent with their own values-belief systems. Thus they not only learned about "material out there", but perhaps even more important, they learned about the "material of themselves".

In this activity, we witnessed the use of all four types of imagery. The deep breathing and opening of the senses provided the background quieting and focusing necessary for sharpening inner perception. The teacher instructed the students to "take time to experience everything" through their five senses. We have found that retention of any cognitive material is greatly enhanced when multi-sensory focusing exercises precede formal learning experiences such as those found in traditional lessons. The cognitive mode was represented by the subject matter itself, "The Raven", and the ideas expressed in the work. The cognitive material is usually found in course outlines, district mandated continua of skills, and textual prescriptions. The affective mode was engaged when the students worked with their inner feelings as symbolized by "dream", "voice of dream", and "message delivered by dream." We see here a heightened sense of self-control, control over one's dream or hypnogogic state of inner perception, inner messages, ability to learn from within and to be the source of one's own advice. The transpersonal mode manifests in the use and recognition of "light", "wisdom" and overall sense of ultimate well-being. The use of all four modes in one lesson made this lesson confluent.

Our intent in using guided imagery for educational purposes is to provide both students and ourselves with the opportunity of using intellectual and symbolic processes, the arts and verbal language for personal explorations within the mind (intrapersonal communication), for increased communication with and insights into others (interpersonal communication), and for a deeper more involved understanding of basic subject matter, academic skills, global concerns, and for processing incoming stimuli from the environment (extrapersonal communication).

We are preparing ourselves to live in a world that calls for an ever increasing knowledge of human capability and human possibility. This includes a sense of competency, an assessment of values and a commitment to the power of individual intelligence working in synergy with the intelligence of others to create a world beneficial to all. Technological skills of the future will be matched with mind skills directing the theatrics of future events. The fabric of the future is being woven from the images and inner visions that we hold in our minds at this very moment. Comments made by a ninth grader after working with our "Inner Space of the Mind" imagery illustrates this idea in a beautiful way.

> It was as if there was no time...no breath...just being. I
> knew I was me...and I could feel a form around me...but
> this form didn't keep me away from other people like a
> body does. I felt like I was one with everyone and

13

everything around me. Peace and love and happiness completely filled me. When the trip ended I felt a little sad because I believe this is how the world is supposed to be. If we can do this in our minds then we should be able to do it in the real world. Maybe we need to think about this more and demand that the world of peace and love that exists in our minds become the real everyday world in which we live.

By examining the responses of students to the imagery activities, it becomes evident that imagery spawns emotional and intellectual awakenings that standard curricula do not. Young people, while exploring the inner space of their own minds in relation to an outside task (such as a cognitive learning objective), add to the growing body of consciousness research by telling of their experiences. These narratives clue us in to heightened dimensions of human possibility, and reveal the powerful new behaviors that are emerging in the repertoire of human behavior.

The following is an example of inner space explored by third graders. Their responses give us insightful information as to what aspects of intellectual performance might be honed and/or sharpened through imagery work.

The children are working with color combinations and have just learned how to get a certain color by mixing and matching various other colors. The teacher directs them to close their eyes, relax, deep breathe and travel away to the "Land of Colors". When they arrive at this land they merge with the various colors and experience themselves and their environment as these colors.

"Close your eyes and take a slow...deep breath...and as you breathe out, remember to breathe out any tiredness...tension...bad feelings you might have at this time(pause)...(Repeat two or three times until children seem centered)...Now look through your magic eye in the center of your forehead and travel away to the land of many colors(pause)...When you arrive at the land of many colors, you will see all kinds of colors - red - orange - yellow - green - blue - purple - and you might even see all kinds of other colors that we haven't even talked about in class...Look around at all these colors...Notice the ones you like the best...See if there are any you don't like as much(pause) ...Now pick one color you like the best and walk right into it and become this color(pause)...What does this color look like?...feel like?(pause)...sound like?...smell like?...taste like?...Does it remind you of anything?(pause)... Now leave this color and choose another color and do the same thing. (Repeat series of questions)...Now walk back into your first color and see what this feels like in your body(pause)...Now do this with your second color and see what happens in your body (pause)...Now have fun and walk through lots of the other colors and see if you can feel any differences in your body(pause)...Stop doing this now, and get ready to return to us here in the room...On the count of three take a slow...deep breath...hold it...and breathe out and feel how relaxed and alert you are(pause)...Do this again...take a slow...deep breath ...hold it...and breathe out and feel how relaxed and alert you are(pause)... Open your eyes, now, and let's share what we experienced in our "Land of Colors"...

Following this journey, the teacher shares his/her own experiences and then invites the children to tell about theirs. Then they draw their "land of color", emphasizing their sensory experiences with each color.

> T. When I went into the yellow, I felt like my body was much bigger and my face started shining like the sun. But when I went into the green I felt cool and thought about how good it feels to walk barefoot through fresh grass. What did some of you feel?
>
> S. It was fun. I liked being blue because it made me feel like the sky where everything is beautiful and free, and there's no one there to bother you.

S. My color was red and I felt hot, kind of like when you're at the beach getting sunburned. But when I was red I could make everything around me feel good. Like my uncle Pete who's sick in the hospital. I visited him when I was all red and he got better when I gave him a shot of my red color. Then I became blue and felt colder.

S. A funny thing happened when I was green. At first I felt like a piece of grass, and an ant walked all over me and it tickled me. Then the ant went away and I felt like I was joining everything else around me - like if everyone was becoming one or something. I could be a tree, a cloud, a bee, even the air when I was green. Then I left the green and went into the yellow and everything became bright and I could see inside everything. People looked real funny with all of their insides showing - like stomachs and bones.

Then the teacher adds an even deeper component to the lesson by asking the children how they are like their color. This enables them to get to know themselves and the others more deeply.

T. How are you like your color?

S. I guess I'm like red when I'm angry or when I make people feel good.

S. I'm like green when I feel good all over and when I feel real close to someone. I feel like blue when I'm happy or dreaming.

BRAIN RESEARCH

Brain research is providing extensive rationale for using visualization and guided imagery activities in education. Among the most popular theories impacting education curricula at this time is that of "right - left brain." Researchers have discovered that the brain's hemispheres seem to process information differently, with the left hemisphere handling the rational, analytical and detailed types of activity and the right hemisphere handling the intuitive, feeling/sensing and holistic types of activity. (Bogen, 1969; Ornstein, 1972; Sperry, 1973; Wittrock, 1981.)

Another theory that has powerful implications for the value of guided imagery is MacLean's "Triune Brain Theory" (1978). His research has shown that we have three brains acting cooperatively with one another. Our oldest brain, the "reptilian", is responsible for all body functions, inherited characteristics, the need for ritual, repetition and learning by imitation. The "limbic" or "mammalian brain" is the seed of emotions, creativity and change. The neo-cortex houses the higher human centers where rational thinking, analysis, conceptualization, creativity, future vision, and transcendent feelings such as oneness of being, ecstasy, synergy or collaboration (rather than competition), peace and ultimate being emerge. The neo-cortex speaks to us through mental pictures, inner images, visions and corresponding sensations, and is the means whereby humans receive insights and intuitions of things to come. These mental images also influence brain and body development and serve as the master plan for human activity.

On a comparative basis, the reptilian brain represents the drive toward rote-repetitive behavior, imitation and modelling. The limbic brain represents stimulus-response, field-dependent, and reward-punishment types of behavior. The neo-cortex represents transcendent, creative, field-independent and self-directed behavior. Imagery work leads to the strengthening of these cortical characteristics.

A third theory related to the value of imagery work is the "holographic" theory proposed by David Bohm (1980). This theory compares the brain to a photographic process called a hologram, where all aspects of an object become visible in its photo. The photo looks alive and multi-dimensional and every part reflects every other part. Bohm believes that every piece of information passing through the brain is connected to every other piece of information and contains the seeds of all other information in it. Although our conscious mind may only perceive a small item of information, a piece of the puzzle, our brain holds all information related to this piece. The brain does this by holding a complete image (the whole picture) of the information being processed. Thus, the more we work with imagery, the easier it is for us to process complex networks of information, and to see wholes rather than isolated parts.

A fourth and very useful theory is that proposed by Leslie Hart (1975). He says that the brain acts on a programmatic basis, and that all of our actions are the results of neural programs directing brain activity. The limbic brain, the seed of emotions, has stored all of our needs, wants, ideas and beliefs. These act as an electro-magnetic force that governs neural activity and decides what actions will ultimately be performed. This force is stored in the brain as a mental picture. Thus, the way to change behavior is to change the images we have about our behavior - to change the pictures in our mind.

CONCLUSION

As we examine the narratives of early people talking about their dreams and visions, as we read stories of geniuses describing how their images and hunches formed the basis of their intellectual endeavors, as scientists admit that their discoveries begin with an inner vision and accompanying feeling or sensation of rightness, as we look at the incredible successes being reported in medicine, psychology and education where imagery work is a central aspect of the curriculum of prescribed activities, as brain research continues to uncover the relationship between mental images, body-mind development and the environment around us, and as we learn to harness the secrets of our own imaging minds, it becomes quite evident that visualization and guided imagery processes are absolutely essential to human growth. Without them we are blind, unable to see and understand either our past heritage or future possibility. We become hapless victims of others' ideas and philosophies, "shoulds" and "hopes" for our lives, and we lose sight of our unique gifts and undertakings in this life. Without inner vision we cannot find our dreams.

Guided imagery is one of the most powerful tools we have for understanding intelligence and harnessing the seemingly unlimited capabilities of the mind. There

18

was a time when the imaging mind heralded the emergence of human forethought, future visioning and planning, and enabled humans to break free from the bonds of imitative instinctual behavior. The time is now when the imaging mind is foraging roads to heightened human intellectual capacities that we are just beginning to understand. It is only when we honor this imaging mind and give it full reign that we will come to a deeper understanding of what our minds in synergistic dialogue with our bodies, emotions and spirit can be and do at best.

What we have learned thus far moves us to encourage the use of visualization and guided imagery in education and counseling types of settings, be these formal (schools, learning centers and offices), or informal (at home, in neighborhoods and social gatherings). We also encourage ongoing research of outcomes so that the benefits of imagery work can be known throughout the world, and practices will continue to be refined and improved. Undoubtedly, our learnings in this regard will not only reveal to us what imagery can accomplish in education, but perhaps even more important, what inner education and significant new learnings take place when imagery activities are used on a regular basis.

CHAPTER TWO

BENEFITS FROM USING IMAGERY

The benefits of using visualization and guided imagery in one's life are many and varied. We have found the following to be most prevalent in our work.

1. Relaxation Helps Learning

We can learn more while relaxed. Tension constricts energy flow into the brain and slows down neural activity, thus making it difficult to think. Many of the neo-cortical brain centers involved in processing information shut down when we are overly stressed or tired. However, when we are relaxed, these centers open up, enabling incoming stimuli (information) to be easily processed.

2. The More We See, the More We Know

"A picture is worth a thousand words." By creating mental pictures and focusing clearly on them, we are actually seeing more of the information coming to us; for example, while reading, it is helpful to create mental pictures of what is being read so that we can comprehend more deeply the material presented in the reading. While listening to a lecture, it helps to create mental pictures of what the speaker is saying so that the conscious mind will see and remember more of what is being said. Once a person trains him or herself to constantly form inner images, all information becomes processed in this imaginative way and expanded learning is constantly taking place.

3. Images and Feelings: The Brain's Way of Knowing

"Thinking in pictures precedes thinking in words." (Kant)

Thoughts are images encoded in feelings that move as electrical vibrations along billions of microscopic neural circuits in the brain. Thus thinking is the continual collaging and re-collaging of these mental images and feelings into comprehensible stories and/or films representing the creation of new information. Creative people often mention how they can sense these "feeling tones" coming over them just before a new idea breaks through into their conscious awareness. Words, oral and or written, emerge from these sensory vibrations and images. Thus they are the least accurate mode for expressing our thoughts. Sensations and images are the territory one experiences, words are but the map. This is why it is difficult to express deeply felt experiences such as oneness, joy and love in words. The words cannot contain the feeling experience in its entirety. Einstein was often quoted as mentioning how his own insights came to him first as feeling tones accompanied by inner visions and images, which he later translated into words.

Scientists frequently report that their discoveries first appear to them in the form of "hunches" or feelings accompanied by inner visions or mental images, and then later reconfigure into verbal patterns or cognitive ideas. Thus all learning is greatly enhanced by learning to recognize and work with feelings and accompanying images. This is why we have noted in our research that communication skills such as oral expression and writing, art, music and drama improve when they are practiced through imagery experiences. We might conclude, then, that when visualization and guided imagery exercises are used on a regular basis, we are actually expanding brain power by developing and refining the natural language forms (feelings and images) of the brain.

4. Opening Up Intuition

Intuition enables us to see the whole, to recognize not only that which is obvious or right before us, but that which is possible to be known. The intuitive mind helps us to fully use both our central and peripheral vision so that at all times we have an expansive view of our lives. We experience life through wide angled lenses, so to speak, which means we are constantly taking in more information and thus we are "knowing more" than ever before. This is what a genius mind does.

Imagery is both the fabric and design of intuition. It is the universal language of direct knowing and direct perception, both of which are aspects of intuitive intelligence. The more we work with our inner visions, learning to understand them and to call on them to give us information that is clearer and more truthful than the often cluttered and biased cognitive mind could possibly offer, the easier it is for us to use our intuition as a guide throughout life. Vaughan, a recognized authority on intuition, describes the relationship between imagery and intuition.

> "Imagery is associated with direct perception ... and can also be a vehicle for profound intuitive insights. Imagery...conveys in an instant feelings and observations which would take many words to describe."
> Awakening Intuition, New York:Anchor/Doubleday, 1979, p. 85)

5. Achieving Self Regulation/Self Mastery

Since images are the root matrix or form for all of our thoughts, we can change ourselves and our environment by changing our images-thoughts. Visualization and guided imagery exercises are being used more frequently for helping individuals gain conscious control over their lives, alter disease patterns, heal physical and emotional illness, change attitudes and behaviors, realize desired goals (such as obtaining jobs, degrees, pay increases), dissipate negative emotions (fear, anxiety, hatred, and the like), and program positive nurturing emotions (joy, abundance, security, trust, love and the like). Biofeedback research has shown that changes in self-image (inner images we hold about ourselves) cause subsequent changes in physical matter. How we think about ourselves (how we picture ourselves) is the pattern of who and what we are.

6. Maintaining Optimal Health

Maintaining a relaxed, centered and confident attitude about onself and the world brings a sense of joy and nurturance to the body. Practicing the various steps to visualization and guided imagery on a regular basis enables one to maintain an overall sense of well-being that contributes to emotional and physical well-being. When we are relaxed and confident about our abilities, blood, which carries oxygen, flows freely through all parts of the body and brain, thus nurturing our nervous system which serves as a receptor for incoming information and a processing unit for thinking.

7. Brain/Mind Power

We know that something exists because we can feel its vibration within us and see it pictured in our mind. Our brains are like highly tuned radio receivers picking up information from the world around us. Thus, the more we develop our powers of visualization and inner imaging, and the more sensitized we become to the action of these feeling images within us, the more information we draw into us. To have an image of something is to know it well. Image = knowledge. Because the very language of the brain/mind consists of vibratory images communicating their essence through feeling tones received by the nervous system, we can say that to develop this imaging ability is to develop brain/mind power.

8. What People Are Saying

We've asked hundreds of people to give us their opinions of guided imagery and what it does for them. The following responses are typical of what many people say.

"I feel relaxed and I remember things better." (Greg, Grade 9)

"I can concentrate better." (Steve, Grade 4)

"My writing has improved." (Andy, Grade 7)

"I can think better and my mind doesn't wander as much." (Tammy, Grade 10)

"Imagery gives me a chance to explore new ideas." (Sharon, Grade 9)

"I can get rid of my stomach aches." (Pamela, Grade 3)

"I don't forget things that I've learned through imagery." (Gail, Grade 12)

"I've learned a lot about my mind and how much control I have over my life."
(Ken, Adult)

"I don't get as tense as I used to." (Mark, Grade 10)

"I feel more peaceful." (Tim, Adult)

"It's easier to make good decisions when you can intuit the outcomes in your mind." (Moira, Adult)

"I feel like everything is OK." (Shawn, Grade 7)

"Imagery makes me feel like somebody, like I'm important." (Meg, Grade 12)

"I can solve my problems with a clearer mind." (Juan, Grade 9)

"It helps me travel to places I've never been and will probably never visit."
(Judy, Grade 6)

"It helps me know myself better." (Kimberly, Grade 11)

"It helps me get rid of my frustrations." (Jason, Grade 10)

"I do a lot better on tests." (Jeremy, Grade 6)

"I feel more knowledgeable when I do imagery." (Jackie, Grade 11)

"I feel like everyone likes me." (Patti, Grade 3)

"Imagery helps us love each other more. We're all good friends." (Sam, Grade 4)

"I feel a lot closer to myself, more comfortable with the unknown within me"
(Ricardo, Adult)

"School work is easier - like spelling and arithmetic." (Tina, Grade 5)

"Everything I do becomes easier if I picture myself doing it successfully."
(Joseph, Grade 11)

"I don't get angry and depressed like I used to." (Peg, Grade 10)

"Imagery helps me be more open-minded and see how others view the world."

(Chris, Adult)

9. What the Research is Saying

A review of the research related to the use of visualization and guided imagery indicates that there is an impressive array of benefits already beginning to surface in both empirical and anecdotal reports. To begin with, the relaxed welcoming atmosphere surrounding imagery work seems to free the flow of creative energy within both teachers and students. This eventually leads to greater academic proficiency. Areas in which this has been established include: increased oral and written communication skills (Galyean, 1982), creative and divergent thinking (Shaw, 1982; Edwards, 1980), vocabulary (Schuster and Martin, 1980), reading achievement (Piccolo and Render, 1982; Steingart and Glock, 1979), social studies achievement (Groff and Render, 1982), test taking skills, I.Q. and handwriting (Toomim, 1982), writing skills (Galyean, 1982; Solanto, 1982) and drawing (Solanto, 1982). These are primarily cognitive gains and are enhanced by non-empirical reports indicating that imagery activities serve to improve spelling, basic computational work and memory skills as well (Galyean, 1982).

Besides these desirable cognitive gains, imagery seems to cause affective gains, such as improved self-esteem (Elligett, Danielson and Holland, 1982), greater motivation, readiness to learn and calmness (Lange, 1982), and self-control (Fugitt, 1982).

A recent study based on observational reports from one hundred and three teachers participating in affective/holistic education projects around the country and in Canada, not only validates the above findings, but adds evidence showing that imagery helps students: (1) be more attentive and less distracted, (2) be more involved in the work being done in class, (3) learn more of the material being taught, (4) enjoy their learning experience more than before imagery was introduced to them, (5) do more original and/or creative work, especially in art and writing, (6) get along better with their classmates, (7) be more kind and helpful to one another, (8) feel more confident, (9) be more relaxed, (10) do better on tests. (Galyean, 1982). Follow-up conversations with several of the respondents also indicated that

25

imagery work enables the students to be more aware of themselves, their own feelings and sensations, body rhythms, preferred ways of learning and be more aware of the feelings and sensations experienced and communicated by others. (Galyean, 1983).

During the last ten years, we have been involved in teaching guided imagery processes to adults as well as to children in both formal and informal learning settings. Besides concurring with the above-cited results, we have noted a tremendous growth in intuitive, metaphoric and extra-sensory intellectual capabilities. People develop the ability to scan their own energy fields detecting areas of tension, discomfort and possible disease, and can do this for each other. They can merge minds and problem solve with great acceleration and ease, and intuit the flow of energy (the way things are going) and prepare themselves to handle situations without stress. Many people develop the ability to dream rich insightful dreams and to interpret their inner visions with great clarity. They find that their richest insights and illuminative experiences come from their inner images and visions, and guide them to make wise choices in life.

All of the effects just cited indicate that guided imagery work is not only beneficial for intellectual growth and academic achievement, but equally as important, for physical, emotional, psychological and spiritual development as well. Imagery work seems to expand and deepen human capabilities on each of these levels. Thus it contributes to the growing repertoire of processes available for improving human life, and for promoting well-being.

CHAPTER THREE

THE PROCESS OF IMAGING

THE BASIC STEPS TO IMAGING

There are six basic steps to effectively using visualization and guided imagery exercises. These are:

> RELAXATION/CENTERING
> FOCUSING
> BODY/SENSORY AWARENESS
> IMAGING
> EXPRESSING/COMMUNICATING
> REFLECTING

1. Relaxing/Centering

A relaxed mind produces clear images. We start by having people get into a relaxed body position, one that will allow oxygen to flow freely throughout the body, and which is most conducive to the person remaining alert throughout the imagery. There are a variety of possibilities, some of which are: (1) sitting in a comfortable chair, spine straight but relaxed, feet flat on the floor, and hands resting comfortably on the thighs or folded softly on the lap; (2) lying face up on a flat but comfortable surface; (3) sitting yoga style with hands resting comfortably on the knees or in the lap; or (4) sitting with head resting on the desk. There is no one position that works "best". We encourage our people to try a variety of these positions and decide which one(s) seem most relaxing to them. It is generally not advisable to have arms, legs or ankles crossed, because this tends to cut off oxygen and create feelings of being cramped. The more relaxed and comfortable a person feels, the more the imagery experience will be enhanced.

Once people are in a relaxed position, we begin with deep breathing exercises ...slowly inhaling...and exhaling..inhaling...and exhaling..inhaling ...and exhaling. We inhale clear light energy...filling every cell in our bodies with light and love...wisdom and knowing...and we exhale any tiredness or tension...distractions or negative thoughts we might be carrying within us.

2. Focusing

When all becomes still within us, when we reach the quiet place of clear reflection, we can see, hear, feel and sense clearly. Focusing exercises help us to sharpen our inner vision and to control our images to work for us. They are like mental visual calisthenics that tune up the mind, clear up inner vision, and give us a sense of mastery and control over inner images. They also help us to think expansively as well as in depth (horizontally as well as vertically), and to see our images in greater detail. The more sharply we focus, taking in both positive and negative space, the more we know. We see what is evident as well as that which isn't evident. The latter serves as the foundation for new knowledge and is a primary characteristic of the genius mind.

3. Body/Sensory Awareness

Each of our senses is involved anytime we feel. Sounds have smells. Textures and images have color tones, tastes and sounds. Each of these sensory systems provides us with information about ourselves and our images. So the more we call upon multi-sensing as a way of knowing things in depth, the more we can learn. We suggest to people that they "see", "hear", "smell", "touch/feel", and "taste" their images, as well as noticing any other subtle sensations surrounding them. Multi-sensing also enlarges the scope of our experience with the images, thus enabling us to learn more from them.

4. Imaging

Once we've learned to relax, center, focus and multi-sense, we are ready for in-depth guided imagery experiences. In some of these experiences we will focus on one or very few images, and in others we will watch lengthy films. Sometimes our images will be still and at other times they will move. We let the images come to us rather than forcing them to appear. If an image doesn't come as a response to a particular suggestion, then we sit quietly with minds at rest waiting for whatever experience is right for us to have. We are the author of our images and they come as wise friends helping us to know more about ourselves, others, the world around us, as well as various types of information such as the subjects we study in school.

At times distractions may float through our minds and temporarily take us away from the images we wish to have. When this happens, recognize that the distractions are there and once again focus on the images that relate to the suggestions in the imagery activity. Soon distractions will become less of a problem.

Sometimes images may appear to be threatening or dangerous. We greet these with love and understanding, asking them what they want from us and what they are trying to tell us. We talk with our images and let them know that they are welcomed into our life only if they remain as helpers. Often an image that appears to be threatening is a friend in disguise and brings us helpful information. It is important to remember that we are always in control of the imagery process.

Watching images pass through us is like watching a movie. We can do two things.

> 1. Remain detached like an objective or outside observer, and see the images as separate from us.
>
> 2. Become one with (or merge with) the images and let ourselves act as the image. We can actually feel the images in our body.
>
> Example: One can watch an elevator go up and down and not feel a thing. Or one can place oneself in an elevator and feel the motion. One can look at a cup of freshly squeezed orange juice and not feel a thing. Or one can picture oneself actually drinking the orange juice and experience the same sensations as if orange juice were really being consumed.

5. Expressing/Communicating

Expressing and communicating are ways of imprinting (not forgetting) the information on our memories. It helps to follow imagery work with a verbal and/or non-verbal mode of expressing what we've experienced. We find that drawing, painting, writing poems, dancing, moving, singing, chanting, sculpting, building, as well as talking about and writing are quite good ways of helping us to remember and learn from our imagery work. Often a fuller understanding of our images comes while we are expressing our experiences in one or a combination of these modes.

Sometimes, though, no matter what we do, a complete understanding of our images doesn't come for days, weeks, months and maybe even years later. Some images stay with us an entire lifetime, guiding us to lead healthy happy lives. If, by chance, some images never seem to make sense to us, we only need to know that they do make sense to the subconscious mind and are working on our behalf from that region of knowing. All that is helpful to us is not always conscious.

I remember a tenth grade girl whom I taught several years ago in a French class. In one of our guided imageries, she received an image of a leafy tree with sharply pointed branches. The tree had a thick trunk and deep roots, and the leaves were deep green. We helped her look at the tree and understand its meaning. She saw the branches as aspects of her own personality. In essence, she recognized that sometimes her temper and "quick tongue" made her seem quite "sharp" to the other kids. On the other hand, her deep roots seemed to represent her values and her commitment to be her own person and follow her conscience.

Friends in the class added their comments to her interpretation and reinforced her own self-understanding; however, it wasn't until six months later that she realized the full impact of this imagery on her life. She had just been elected student body treasurer. At one of the student meetings, she lost her temper and openly criticized another student. Her words were sharp, unfair and unjustified. Suddenly, in the midst of this noxious outburst, one of her good friends said: "Hey, remember your tree! You had lots of soft green leaves as well as those sharp branches!" With that the girl stopped, laughed and apologized to the other girl. She then restated her criticisms in a way that was gentle, firm and fair to all concerned. She mentioned to me that whenever she would start to become "sharp tongued" and unjustly critical of others, she would remember "her tree" and it would help soften her feelings. This story illustrates quite well the idea that our images are good friends and speak to us whenever we need their help.

6. Reflecting

We encourage people to reflect upon the meaning of their imagery experiences such as you saw evidenced in the example given for #5. Often we find that deep insights into personality, inner resources and strengths, cosmic and universal energies, emotional influences and intellectual capabilities are brought about through contemplative examination of inner images.

WHAT IF I DON'T SEE ANYTHING?

There are three types of imagery: audio, visual, and kinesthetic. We experience all three simultaneously, but often aren't aware of this and may believe that we "don't image" because we don't actually "see" images in front of our eyes. Those who are new at working with inner imagery may find that one mode predominates over the others. That's why it's important to tell your people that some of us actually "see" vivid pictures in front of us, some of us hear quite audible sounds, while others feel the images in our bodies. And some of us combine two or more modes depending on the imagery stimulus. Taste and smell are also also aspects of imaging and relate to kinesthetic processing of information. Lead your people in the following exercise to learn more about how they image.

L. Close your eyes and listen to these words. Notice if you
- actually see the picture in your mind's eye
- hear a sound (or sounds) associated with the words
- feel the words in your body
- smell or taste the words
- think about the words but don't actually see, hear, feel, smell or taste the words.

OCEAN   (Lake, River)
FRIEND
SNAKE
PIZZA
ROCK MUSIC

POPCORN

RUNNING (Climbing Stairs/Crawling on Knees)

ELEVATOR

RAIN

LEMON (Orange, Grapefruit, Strawberries, Apple)

After your people have gone through the list and indicated how they experienced each word, you might want to give them the list a second time and suggest that they experience each word multisensorially.

> Example: L. OCEAN
> "Picture the ocean in front of you. Smell the
> salty air. Taste the salt water on your lips. Throw
> the water on your face. What does it feel like?
> Now step into the water. What does it feel like?
> Look around and see who or what else is around the
> water. Then listen for any sounds. Now dive in and
> go for a swim. What does this feel like?

Once you have introduced your people to multisensory experiencing, the process becomes natural for them whenever they work with visualization and guided imagery. This helps them to more fully experience their images and to receive more information from them.

In case you have some people who believe they can't image no matter what you say, you might try the following exercise. I have found even the most persistent resisters tend to "give in" and admit that "they do image, after all". The purpose of this exercise is to show how the imaging mind manifests itself in bodily responses.

> L. Close your eyes and picture yourself biting into a sour
> lemon. What does this feel like on the tip of your tongue?
> On your teeth? In your throat?

> What happens when someone scratches the blackboard with
> a long finger nail? Imagine this is happening to you right
> now.

You're at the top of a thirty story building leaning over the rail watching cars and people below. Someone comes up from behind you and gives you a gentle shove. What happens?

Ask people to notice any bodily sensations they experience from these images. The presence of bodily responses "proves" the existence of these images since the actual physical stimuli are not present.

Note: You might also lead them in the exercise "Designing Your Own Imagery Journey" in the chapter Getting Started.

CHAPTER FOUR

MAKING MIND SIGHT WORK FOR YOU

HOW TO USE THIS BOOK

The following suggestions may be helpful to you when you first begin working with Mind Sight. We encourage you to follow your own intuitive wisdom in deciding how to merge Mind Sight with your own particular situation.

1. Read the Imagery Activities Verbatim or Adapt as Needed

You can either read the imageries verbatim from our scripts or adapt them for your own purposes. In either case, make sure to familiarize yourself with the imagery prior to using it. Be aware of the language level used. The imagery activities in Mind Sight are worded in a way general enough that you can use them for most age groups. However, in some cases you may find the wording too simplistic or too difficult depending upon the age level(s) of the group you are working with. If this happens, reword them accordingly. Also, we have not intended these scripts to be all-inclusive. It will often be appropriate for you to elaborate upon the basic ideas contained in the imagery. The age level of your group and your objectives in using the imagery will suggest when you should embellish the suggestions contained in various imageries.

Our research has shown that people who lead guided imageries on a regular basis, tend to avoid "recipe approaches" to this work. It was not the intention in Mind Sight to write an imagery activity and then specify that it is for a certain age or grade level, but rather to give the reader a feel for how the imagery could progress. Teachers, parents, counselors, therapists, anyone using these imageries, should adapt the written scripts to fit the interests, maturity and readiness levels of those working with them.

2. Beginning the Imageries

We always begin imagery work with deep breathing/centering exercises, such as those presented in the Getting Started section. We suggest you familiarize yourself with the variety of breathing exercises we've presented and use these on a consistent basis, or create a form that works well for you.

Note: Most of the imageries in Mind Sight begin with the actual text of the imagery and do not include the deep breathing/centering aspects. We have found that the deep breathing/centering is easy to master, and after people have led a few imageries, they do not need the breathing/centering form repeated in each imagery script. The same is also true for bringing your people out of an imagery exercise.

3. Length of Pauses

In some cases we have structured the length of a pause by saying "You have one minute of clocktime...". The shorter pauses marked by (pause) are usually about 10 seconds. While people are experiencing aspects of their journeys such as "exploring a land" or "looking at, listening to and feeling objects", you might need to give a full minute or two for the experience. It's a good idea to ask your people if they had enough time (too much or too little) to comfortably experience their imagery. Use their feedback as a gauge for timing the activities. You might also prefer to pause in places other than those we have indicated. Do whatever feels best to you.

4. Suggestions for Working with Beginners

When people are first beginning to experience visualization and guided imagery work, we have found it is better to give them many detailed directions and talk them through the experience rather than giving them fewer suggestions and expecting them to fill in the details on their own. (Of course there are always individuals who are exceptions to this observation.) Beginners often tend to lose their images to distractions or thoughts that are unrelated to the imagery experience itself. We suggest the following as an adequate model for presenting imagery activities to beginners.

L. Close your eyes and take a slow...deep breath...hold it...now exhale any tiredness, tension or distractions you might be feeling at this time (pause 10 sec.)...Take another deep breath, only this time exhale with a slight sigh and let your body feel yourself getting rid of annoying thoughts, distractions and/or feelings of tiredness (pause 10 sec.)...(Repeat deep breathing two or three more times until you sense the group is quite relaxed.) Now imagine you are lying in the sun...a very warm...mellow ...friendly sun...It's rays are slowly penetrating through your skin...making you feel deeply relaxed...You can feel this warmth all the way to your bones (pause 10 sec.)...Are you lying on your back?...your stomach?...your side?...How are you lying at this time?... (pause 10 sec.). If you need to put some sun tan oil on you do so at this time. (pause 5 sec.)...Listen carefully to the sounds around you. What do you hear?...Can you hear the gentle wind?...other people's voices? Where are you at this time?..at a park?...at the beach?...at a lake or river?...on the grass in your yard?...on a sun deck?...in a lounge chair? (pause 10 sec.)...Suddenly you smell something delicious...a food that you love to eat...What is this food? (pause 10 sec.)...Is it in a snack bar?...someone's picnic?... Are you able to go over and eat some of this food?...or must you be content to just smell it? (pause 5 sec.)...If you are able to eat some of it do so at this time. Enjoy every bite...If you aren't able to eat it, just enjoy the delicious smells and note how your body responds to these smells of a favorite food (pause 10 sec.)...Now let the images of this food and the delicious smells go away and concentrate once again on how good it feels to lie in the sun and feel the sun's friendly warmth penetrate deep into your body making you feel deeply relaxed (pause 10 sec.)...Keep this pleasant feeling with you all day. Prepare yourself to return to us here in this room (place, space, etc.) fully alert, refreshed and ready to work with our experiences...On the count of three, take a slow...deep breath...hold it...and exhale with a slight sigh...Open your eyes and stretch your arms and legs...wiggle your fingers and toes...rub your face and stomach and feel the life (vitality) and strength in your body...

Note: If any of your people seem spacey, have them stand and shake the energy from their legs and arms, feet and hands. They can also rub their eyes, arms, shoulders, or rub their hands together, whatever will ground them. Consult the section entitled Settling Down for further suggestions.

We also suggest that you follow this activity with an art, poetry, music, drama, movement, written, and/or oral expressive activity so that people can share each other's experiences.

5. Working with More Experienced Imagers

Once individuals are accustomed to working with inner imagery and can adequately clear their minds of distractions and unwanted thoughts, and can form images at will, they do not need suggestions to be as detailed as beginners do. These people are capable of taking a basic theme and creating in free float fashion any images they need to better understand and learn from the basic image theme. The following example provides an adequate model of working with the more experienced imagers.

L. Repeat deep breathing as in example for "Beginners"; however, some of your people may already be using a form a deep breathing that differs from the ones suggested in Mind Sight. Invite them to use whatever form feels best to them. Begin with "Imagine you are lying in the sun feeling the warmth and friendliness of the rays penetrating gently through your skin...relaxing you and making you feel good all over (pause 10 sec.)...While you are lying here in the sun you become aware of much peace and beauty around you...There are some beautiful sounds that you like to hear...and there are some delicious smells that make your mouth water...You feel a deep calm and joy as you experience this moment...You have two minutes of clock time which is all the time you need to fully enjoy this experience (pause two minutes)...Bring this experience to completion and keep these pleasant feelings with you all day (pause 10 sec.) ...Now focus your attention on your physical body...and feelings in your body...and become aware of the sounds and vibrations in this room (pause 5 sec.)...On the count of three..."(Continue in same manner as for "Beginners")...

Note: At conclusion of imagery have your people express in art, music, writing, poetry, movement, drama, or oral expression the content of their experiences. In this way both you and they can see how you've each experienced the imagery work. The purpose is not to have each person experience the imagery in the same way, but rather to encourage each person to make full use of the unique way in which their imaging mind communicates to them.

6. Bringing People Out of the Imagery Experience

We have also provided you with a variety of ways for bringing your people out of the imagery experience. Find the mode that you like best and use this one consistently. Or experiment with several modes. The basic idea is to give people a chance to slowly leave the place of their inner journey, while gradually reconnecting with the physical environment of their bodies, the room (space, place) where the imagery is taking place and others around them. There is no "one way" to do this; thus we have provided you with several variations.

Note: Most of the imageries in Mind Sight do not include a form for bringing your people out of the experience. Familiarize yourself with the section Getting Started and use these forms (or your own version). We've found that after people have led a few imagery journeys, they no longer need to see a form for closing the exercise written into the imagery scripts.

7. Follow Up Discussions and Activities

For most of the imagery activities we have included topics for discussion and follow up activities. We have found that the imagery work is deepened through the sharing and comparing of experiences as well as through insights spawned by the follow up activities. We recommend that you expand these topics and follow up activities to include creative ideas of your own.

8. Using Music to Enhance the Imagery Experiences

Sometimes the imageries are enhanced by the addition of appropriate music. Although we have presented you with some of our favorite selections, the list is limited. We suggest you look for music that helps you have deeper, more moving experiences with the imageries and use these selections as the basis for your own work.

9. Samples of Work Done with Guided Imagery Activities

Whenever you see this symbol you are looking at work produced by an individual who had been working with the guided imagery indicated on that page. The samples we have selected are not meant to be typical of a particular age group, grade level, nor are they meant to illustrate what "should happen" when imagery work is done well. Rather they illustrate what has "actually happened" in some of the settings where guided imagery has been done on a regular basis. The examples were taken from kindergarten through adult level classes and groups, from individual counseling sessions, workshop experiences and family gatherings. They represent a wide diversity of proficiency levels, readiness and prior experience.

A WORD TO COUNSELORS AND THERAPISTS

You are probably working in a less formal educational setting where you, in collaboration with your clients, co-determine the goals and objectives of the learning encounters. You are not bound by predetermined learning objectives or prescribed curriculum. Affective and transpersonal goals are usually more central to your work than cognitive goals because the people coming to work with you are interested in their emotional and spiritual growth as well as their intellectual development. If, however, you are working with intellectual cognitive goals, then you might wish to use the Guided Cognitive Imageries as well as the Guided Affective and Transpersonal Imageries.

Assess Needs and Wants

Find out what your people need and want from the therapeutic encounter with you. Get a feel for the inner material they are dealing with. What psychological, psychic and/or spiritual themes are they dealing with? This may take time, discussion and intuitive insight on your part.

Select Appropriate Imagery Activity

Select one or more of the affective and/or transpersonal imageries that corresponds to these needs, wants and themes. (In some cases you may wish to rewrite or adapt the imagery to your specific needs.) For example, let's suppose an individual comes to you for help. The person has very little self-confidence, and views him or herself as a failure. You might select the affective imagery "Tree" to get them in touch with how negatively they view themselves. Then you would have them do "Successful Me" and, perhaps, "Passing Tests" to show them how to change these negative scripts to positive ones.

Decide Your Objectives

Be aware of what goals and objectives you and those working with you wish to accomplish. Select your imageries in view of these goals and objectives. For example, your people may need or want to experience a mind merge (mental synergy) where they have instant, all-embracing communication with each other. You would lead them in the transpersonal imagery "Merging Energies" where they experience what it is like to unite with each other via energy expansion. Or you may have an individual or group of people who tend to look at the negative side of life and need to develop the skill of positive thinking. You would have them experience the affective imagery "Happy Thoughts". Others may feel like victims of circumstance, often referred to as the "poor me" syndrome. You might present them with the affective imageries "Changing Unwanted Feelings" and/or "I am Not My Problems".

Note Results

Be sure to note what positive effects or new avenues of growth and possibility open for your people as a result of their imagery work. Call attention to any desired changes that seem to be occurring because of the imagery activities. For example, if the person working with you lacks self-confidence, you would point out any of their images that show the potential for self-confidence. If they are working with the affective imagery "Tree", they might have described the tree as "small, graceful, having fragile branches but deep roots." You could point out that although the tree might look feeble on the outside, it is deeply rooted and cannot be moved against its will. Its smallness has nothing to do with its strength. In fact, its smallness probably helps it be non- threatening to people. It has a hidden strength. Then you might lead the person to discover some of their hidden strengths.

Suggested Follow-Through Activities

After you and your people have reflected upon your experiences, noting results and freshly gathered insights, decide where you would like to go with this information. This follow-up may take the form of: (1) listening to a tape of the imagery and continuing to use it on a regular basis in one's personal life, (2) writing thoughts in a journal, (3) drawing or painting insights, or (4) meeting in small discussion groups to share growth experiences. Trust your intuitive wisdom to guide you in suggesting appropriate follow-up activities for yourself and your people. Often your students, clients, family or others working with you will have excellent ideas for follow-up activities.

A WORD TO PARENTS

You can use the activities in Mind Sight in practically all of the ways suggested for educators, counselors and therapists. You are most likely working at home with your family in an informal "as we are" environment. Thus you have a wonderful opportunity to "raise your family" with the feeling that visualization and guided imagery is a natural tool for expanding human capabilities on all levels of physical, emotional, intellectual and spiritual awareness. With your guidance, your children and their friends may enthusiastically accept visualization and guided imagery exercises as a natural and necessary rubric in their daily lives.

Deciding Which Imagery Activities to Use

Determine what you and your family need and/or want to know or do. Then select those imagery activities that best respond to these needs and wants. For example, you might want all family members to get to know each other more deeply and to honor the unique characteristics of each person. You select the affective imageries "I am Unique" and "Personalities" and invite each person to participate in and share their experiences from these imageries. On the other hand you may find that communication has broken down and you need to clear up misunderstandings, so you work with the affective imagery "Needs and Wants" and/or the transpersonal imagery "Working Out Conflict". If your children are having difficulty with spelling, you might have them work with the cognitive imagery on "Spelling". Or perhaps you and your family are interested in exploring expanded human capabilities and energy fields, so you would select the transpersonal imagery "Body/Mind Connections".

Sometimes you may not have a consciously-perceived reason for wanting to experience a particular imagery. You may just "feel right" about a particular activity. Trust your intuitive wisdom in this regard and carefully observe what happens, what benefits you and family members experience from working with the imagery.

Follow-Up Activities for the Family

Some families follow their imageries with art amd poetry types of activities or story writing. These are then displayed in places of honor around the house so that family members and friends can all share in the insights and learnings.

How One Parent Used Imagery to Help Her Daughter with a Homework Assignment

A few weeks after I had given a demonstration on the use of guided imagery with kids to a group of interested parents, one parent wrote to tell me how she had used one of my imageries to help her daughter with a homework assignment.

Her daughter came home from school one afternoon disgruntled that she had to write a composition about Abraham Lincoln. She told her mom that "Lincoln is dead so who cares what he did a long time ago." The mother suggested that her daughter close her eyes and imagine herself to be Lincoln standing before hundreds of people about to deliver the Gettysburg Address. "The people are anxiously awaiting to hear what you will say about freedom, slavery, and equal rights. Some are favorable to your ideas whereas others are openly hostile. You have your own convictions. Are you strong enough to stand by them, or will you give in to popular opinion? What are your thoughts as you stand before these people? Are you afraid? Confident? As you look into the crowd, can you see the faces of your friends? Of your enemies? You've just finished your talk. Is there applause? Are there boos? What do people say about you now?" The mother then had her daughter write down her experiences with the imagery journey. The girl wrote enthusiastically for over an hour and told her mother that "writing has never been so much fun" and that "I never knew Lincoln had such feeling for poor people." She received an "A" on her paper.

CHAPTER FIVE

BEFORE YOU BEGIN, REMEMBER TO . . .

As you begin to use visualization and guided imagery, keep the following points in mind. They will help your use of imageries to be more thorough, long-lasting and rewarding.

1. Tell your people a few things about visualization and guided imagery:
   - what it is
   - how it works
   - why it is important
   - how people use it
   - what are some of the results

   Note: See the chapter <u>The Imaging Mind</u> for background material on the theory and practice of visualization and guided imagery, as well as research results. The section on <u>Benefits</u> will also be helpful to you.

2. Tell them stories related to your own use of visualization and guided imagery. Perhaps you have taken part in courses, workshops or seminars where you worked with imagery activities and had some significant experiences to share with others. We have found that people tend to respond quite well to imagery work when the person leading the guided imagery is willing to share his/her own personal experiences.

3. Invite your students to participate in the activities. <u>Voluntarism</u> is our <u>foremost rule</u>. No one is ever forced or cajoled into participating. Alternate work or tasks are given those who prefer not to participate.

   Note: If you have some people who prefer not to participate, you might ask them to move to the back of the room or work in another area of the room. This enables you to keep your imagery group together, while providing the others with a place where they can comfortably observe the imagery work and, if they wish, do it on their own at a distance from the others. We have found that people who are hesitant to engage in imagery work often ask to participate after they've had the opportunity to first observe the activities.

4. Provide for movement exercises such as stretching, jumping, running in place, stomping and dancing for those people who have too much energy at the time you want to begin the imagery activity. We find that energy brush downs, shaking off excess energy or feelings, dancing out nervousness, hyperactivity and the like, help settle all of us into the quieter imagery work.

If some of your younger people seem wiggly or giggly, have them sit next to or in front of you where you can put your arm around them, or can place your hand gently on their shoulders, or on their back between the shoulder blades.

Note: See the section entitled Settling Down for ideas on brush downs and shaking off excess energy.

5. Teach your people deep breathing exercises before doing the visualization and guided imagery activities with them. This will help them perceive their inner images with greater clarity (less distraction) and will prepare them to receive information in greater depth.

Note: Deep breathing exercises are included in the

45

chapter <u>Getting Started</u>.

6.   Since visualization and guided imagery work calls for a quiet, undistracted mind and clear mental screen, it is helpful to keep the eyes closed during the imagery exercises. When the eyes are open, thousands of images flash on the retina and optical nerves making it difficult for the brain to sort out the outer and inner images. However if some of your people are afraid to close their eyes, have them first image with eyes open. As they become more
comfortable with imagery work, encourage them to close their eyes.

Note: Open eye exercises are included in the chapter <u>Getting Started</u>.

7.   Work from specific learning objectives and evaluate outcomes. Your people need to know why they are doing a certain activity and how it fits into the lesson or task for the day. For example, if you notice that your people have been uncooperative with each other, you might suggest that they work with the <u>Guided Affective Imageries</u> on "Love", "Paint with Love", "Love Circle" and/or "Appreciation". Tell them that imageries will help them care for, feel appreciated by and cooperate better with each other. This helps them to know why they are doing the imagery activity and what might be an expected outcome.

8.   Carefully monitor people's responses to the imagery work. Notice if some people become frightened or tend to "space out". Although these are rare occurrences, if this does happen, tell your people that whatever they experience is "OK" and that they never need fear their inner experiences. We are always in control of our images and can change frightening or uncomfortable images to helpful, friendly ones.

I remember working with a group of fourth graders where a boy traveled into a forest and met a horrid-looking monster. The monster threatened to eat him up. The boy opened his eyes and told me he never wanted to go into the forest again because it was full of terrible monsters. I gently hugged him and told him that sometimes I, too, saw monsters in my forest, and that my monsters became friendly when I talked with them. I told him how monsters were creatures who thought no one loved them and when they found someone who would love them, they would change into loving, friendly creatures.

Then we talked about using our own loving energy to change negative or frightening images to helpful, friendly ones. I had everyone close their eyes and picture themselves in a strong glass bubble, or behind a protective shield. Then we went on a "monster hunt" where we found a monster and confronted it from behind our protective screen. We told the monster that we welcomed it to stay with us but only if it would be a loving helpful companion. We promised to care for it, talk with it and make it feel wanted and loved. Then we watched to see what the monster would do.

Some of the kids reported that their monsters changed into beautiful horses, dogs, cats and the like. Others said that their monsters cried and felt loved for the first time. Some monsters went away. In any case, the kids saw how their attitudes were the key to changing the frightening monsters into friendly ones. The boy was able to meet his monster, pet it, feed it and talk to it. He reported later that his monster had told him that he felt very lonely and ugly and that he didn't know how to treat other people kindly. The boy promised to treat him like a friend and the monster suddenly became "shiny like the sun" and "said he would be my friend and help me with my homework."

Another aspect of monitorship is noting the rhythm, tone and speed with which you lead the activities. Check often with your people to find out if they were able to follow you with ease. Sometimes they will make suggestions such as "slow down", "go a little faster", "we need longer pauses", "the music was too loud", "the imagery was too long (or short)".

We have found that individuals differ in their needs and preferences regarding imagery work and the best way to continually refine methods and practices is to ask your group for feedback on a regular basis.

9. At all times validate and appreciate everyone's unique experiences. Everyone is "right" and all imagery trips are "successful ventures." Honor the individuality expressed in the imagery experiences and encourage your people to learn from each other. By listening to each other's stories and looking at each person's expression of inner work, we gain deeper insight into human capability and human possibility.

10. Provide for follow-up activities such as art, painting, drawing, moving, dancing,

dramatizing, poetry, creative writing and expression, songs and music, and oral discussion to reinforce, recreate and express the imagery experiences.

11. Invite others to write and/or lead imagery activities when they feel ready. Some of the best imagery work I've seen has come from student-led or participant-led imageries.

12. If you are working in a formal education setting, inform your administration, fellow faculty and parents of the value of imagery work. Share with them your successes and solicit their support for your work.

13. Be sure to find out the needs and preferences of your local community (i.e., parents, students, peers, etc.) regarding the types of imageries that are deemed appropriate to use in your specific setting. Some groups may wish that imagery be used only for relaxation purposes, others for cognitive gains, and still others for transpersonal development.

> Note: In some texts on guided imagery we find the term "meditation" used synonymously with the term "guided imagery". Meditation as used in imagery work refers to the process of undistracted focusing on inner images and feelings. It is not to be confused with the religious connotation of "meditation" which refers to the act of prayer.

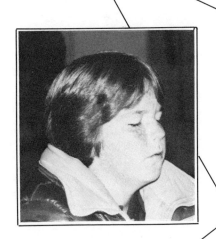
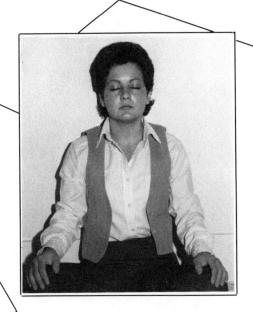

Look
within
to see the
miracle
you are!

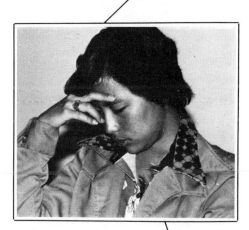
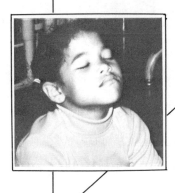

Mind Sight
learning through imaging

CHAPTER SIX

GETTING STARTED

Very often people ask "How do I start?" First of all, note the energy level of your group. If energy is too high or overly active, lead your people in one or more of the "Settling Down" exercises we've included in this section. If you have some people who are fearful of closing their eyes you might want to begin by having them do some of the "Open Eye" exercises.

Once your group seems ready to begin, start with the "Deep Breathing" and "Centering" exercises that clear the mind of distractions that hinder the ability to image clearly. Then acquaint them with the "Focusing" exercises that sharpen inner perception and help us to control our images. We use the "Focusing" exercises whenever people find it difficult to slow their thought processes sufficiently enough to examine their images in detail.

When your people have learned these "basics", you can them lead them in the easy to follow "Sensory Imageries" we have prepared for beginners. These imageries are loaded with a variety of pleasant easy to experience sensory stimuli that are processed with all of the senses. Once your people have learned to image with all of their senses, and to focus undistractedly on their images and feelings, they are ready to fully experience the more expansive cognitive, affective and transpersonal imageries.

> Note: Although the imageries in this section are relatively simple, we have found that they often spark profound personal insights. See the example of participant work provided for "A Special Place" to illustrate the depth with which some people experience these activities. We recommend that, even if your people are not beginners and are comfortable with the longer cognitive, affective and transpersonal imageries, you consider using the thematic ones presented in this section for their ability to initiate profound personal experiences.

SETTLING DOWN EXERCISES

The following exercises are helpful whenever people are feeling "wound up", hyper, and unable to settle down into the quieter centering and focusing activities.

1. <u>Shaking Off Excess Energy</u>

   a) Start shaking one foot and continue shaking the leg, thighs, hips and buttocks, arms, hands, shoulders and face on that side of the body. Then continue down the other side. Imagine yourself shaking off any excess energy or unwanted feelings such as anger, fear, excitement and the like.

   b) Stand inside a circle (made from string, chalk, hula hoop, etc.) and jump up and down until you jump out of the unwanted feelings of anger, fear, excitement, nervousness. You might want to limit the time spent inside this circle by saying "You have thirty seconds (one minute, etc.) which is all the time you need to jump out of the feelings you don't want to have at this time."

c) Do calisthenics like touching toes, jumping jacks, squats, twists and turns and running in place. Note: It helps to play energizing music in the background and then switch to more soothing, restful music. After completing the calisthenics, have your people deep breathe to soothing music.

d) Dance or move to restful meditative music.

2. <u>Massage</u>

Have your people give each other light shoulder, back, neck and/or facial massages. Doing this to the rhythm of soothing meditative music is very effective. If, however, the group is lethargic and you wish them to have more energy, change to music of a faster rhythm.

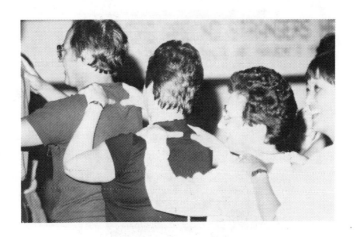

3. <u>Brush Downs</u>

Work with a partner. One of you is the giver and the other is the receiver. Place your hands on the crown of your partner's head and imagine sending him or her feelings of peace, trust and love. Gently stroke down each side of the temples, ears, face, shoulders, arms and hands, hips, legs, ankles and feet. Repeat four or five times until your partner feels these calming vibrations.

You can also brush down the front and back of the person. Be sure to keep the image of yourself sending your partner feelings of peace, trust and love.

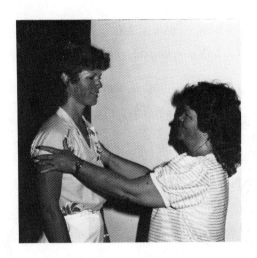

4. Spine Brush

Place two fingers on each side of the spine starting at the tip of the spine. Gently but firmly stroke down each side all the way to the small of the back. Repeat five or six times or as needed to calm the nervous system.

To energize your partner, stroke up the spine. This stimulates the nerves.

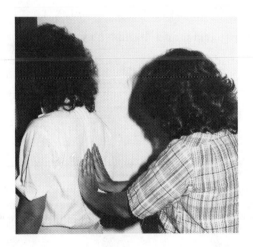

5. Touch for Health

These exercises, developed by Dr. John Thie and his associates, are based on the Chinese theories of energy meridians in the body. These meridians carry energy to all parts of the body and whenever there is a blockage or imbalance, we feel pain, discomfort or disease. By learning to map out and apply pressure to the points of release along these meridians, we can reduce stress, nervousness, physical and emotional discomfort, distraction and fatigue.

Resource: J. Thie, <u>Touch for Health,</u> (THEnterprises, PO Box 751-C, 1184 N. Lake Avenue, Pasadena, CA 91104.)

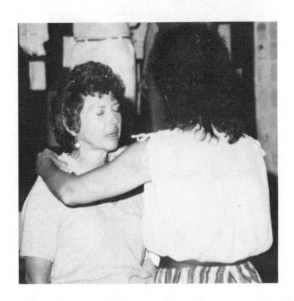

6. <u>Mirroring Game</u>

Work with a partner. One person is the leader and the other the "mirror". The leader gently moves his or her hands and arms, and the "mirror" imitates these movements. It helps to play soothing music in the background. After arms and hands have been "mirrored", the leader can then move shoulders, neck, face, hips, legs and feet and the "mirror" continues to imitate the movements.

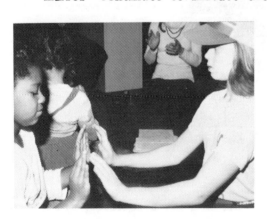

7. Acupressure Massage

   Place one or two fingers in the center of your forehead and rub
   gently in a circular fashion. Then move to the temples and continue
   rubbing in a circular fashion. The circles should be one half to one
   inch in diameter. Then move to the eyebrows and gently place your
   thumbs under your eyebrow bone and stroke from the nose to the
   temples. Then place your palms over your open eyes and block out all
   light. Look into the darkness and let your eyes float peacefully in this
   darkness. Deep breathe while letting your eyes float. Do each of the
   steps about one minute before moving on to the next one.

OPEN EYE EXERCISES

Doing "open eye" short imaginative exercises is an excellent preparation for deeper guided imagery work. You can also use these "open eye" exercises with people who are afraid of closing their eyes.

Now and then you may have a few people who do not believe they actually image. Or they may ask you to explain how imagery works. If this happens, we suggest you lead these people through the exercise in this section entitled "Designing Your Own Imagery Journey".

Exercises in this section are sequentially arranged from simple to more complex.

BEFORE YOU BEGIN, PLEASE REMEMBER TO ...

- ☐ Prepare your people by discussing the importance of using the particular imagery at this time.

- ☐ Check to see if they need any movement types of activities to help settle and center their energy.

- ☐ Check to see if they need a focusing activity to sharpen their inner vision.

- ☐ Make alternate work available in case you have individuals who do not want to do the imagery activity.

- ☐ Prepare any needed materials such as crayons, paints, paper ahead of time.

- ☐ Read the imagery in its entirety and change the wording and pauses to meet the maturity, readiness, interest and proficiency levels of your group.

- ☐ Include a deep breathing/centering exercise to begin the imagery.

- ☐ If the imagery does not include a form for ending the activity (i.e., the "countdown and return to the room"), be sure you have one ready. You can look at the chapter on Getting Started for ideas.

- ☐ Consider adding multi-sensory suggestions such as "What do you see?...hear?...feel?...smell?...taste? ..." whenever you wish to heighten the sensory experience even if they are not included in the actual text of the imagery.

MOUSE

IMAGERY:

Look at the floor...and imagine you see a brown mouse
on the floor(pause)...Now the mouse runs across the
floor and under a chair(pause)...Now the mouse runs
from under the chair to the corner(pause)...Now the
mouse runs up the wall all the way to the ceiling
(pause)...and just as the mouse reaches the ceiling
you see a ...oh my heavens!!...it's a green mouse
(pause)...The two mice run across the ceiling together
and they find another mouse that is brown and green
striped(pause)...Do you think this mouse is related
to the first two?(pause)...All three mice run down
the wall and onto the floor...and finally they
disappear under a chair(pause)...You wait for them
to come out but they don't come out(pause)...Suddenly
the brown mouse emerges but the green, and green and
brown mice don't(pause)...You look under the chair and
there are no mice under the chair(pause)...This puzzles
you and as you are thinking about what might have
happened you look up at the ceiling...and there you
see the green mouse talking with the green and brown
mouse(pause)...And then they disappear...

DISCUSSION:

Do you think the green and brown mouse was related to
the other two?
How did the two mice get from the chair to the ceiling?
What happened to the brown mouse?

NOTE:

We are indebted to Violet Oaklander for the basic idea of
this imagery.

STRETCHING IMAGINATIONS

PREPARATION:

Tell your people that they will use an imagery activity to visualize and create a "Heffalump".

MATERIALS:

Colored pens, crayons, pastels or chalk and paper.

IMAGERY:

Imagine that you are seeing a Heffalump for the first time ... It may be a mythological creature ... a machine ... an animal combining qualities of several animals ... any shape that you may imagine (pause) ... Notice the color ... size ... texture form ... of the Heffalump (pause) ... Notice the function of the Heffalump (pause) ... When you are ready ... open your eyes and draw the Heffalump that you have seen ...

DISCUSSION: (After the drawing is completed)
Describe your "Heffalump"
How is it helpful to you?
To others?
Is the world ready for your "Heffalump"?
Does it cost anything to make/create it?
Where does it live?

Michael (Grade 2)

A LEMON-INSTEAD OF AN ORANGE

IMAGERY:

Imagine yourself being in a room...the room is sort
of dark...You remember that there is a basket of fresh
juicy oranges on the table and you feel like eating
one...So you reach over...take one...peel it...and take
a big bite...just waiting for the sugary sweet taste of
the juicy pulp...But someone switched the oranges to
lemons and you just bit into a sour...very sour...lemon
(pause)...What's happening in your mouth?...on your
teeth and tongue(pause)...

DISCUSSION:

Describe what happened? What did your mouth do? Your lips?
Etc.

When you think about eating a lemon what happens in your
body? (Point out that if they couldn't actually "see" the lemon
they wouldn't have had this reaction.)

61

YOUR HOME

(Be attentive to note cultural differences in designing this visualization)

IMAGERY:

> Think about your home...where you live...Do you live in a house...apartment...trailer...mobile home...cabin?(pause) ...What does it look like?(pause)...Walk around the outside and look at it...Note the structure...paint...landscape such as grass...flowers...trees...rocks...sand...and anything else that is there(pause)...Now go inside and carefully examine the first room you enter...Notice everything in the room such as table...chairs...sofa...rug... television...magazines...pictures...lamps(pause)...Now look at the kitchen...What do you see?(pause)...(Continue for each room in the house.)

DISCUSSION:

> Describe your place to us. What did you see outside? Inside? Are there any changes you would like to make?
> Once your people have done this, point out that they needed to "see" this place in order to describe it. Once they hear you say this, they usually feel better about their ability to visualize in their mind's eye.

"The color of the house was white. White is beautiful because it is the color of clouds. Brown is the ground and tree trunks. It is God's favorite, because he likes brown. Orange is the color of oranges and orange makes me feel good. Red is the flowers. Roses and apples are red. Red is beautiful like my heart and strawberries. Yellow is the sun shining. Yellow is nice shining windows. It is the color of lemons. It makes me feel beautiful and shining." (Eric's house was painted in brown, orange, red and yellow and outlined in white.)

Eric (Grade 1)

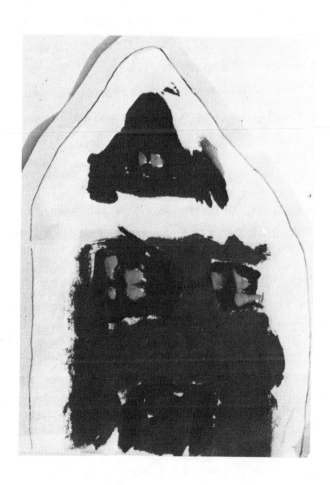

APPLE

IMAGERY:

Think of an apple...and make it any kind...color...
shape you wish(pause)...What kind is it...or do you
know?(pause)...What color is it?(pause)...What shape...
such as round...oval...square?(pause)...Notice if it
is hard...or soft(pause)...Do you see any finger marks...
bruises...blemishes?...

DISCUSSION:

What does your apple look like? Describe it in detail.
(Once your people can do this, you point out that they
have, indeed, "seen" an apple in their mind or they
wouldn't have been able to describe it. When they hear
you say this, they usually feel better about their
ability to visualize...to see in their mind's eye.)

"I am a shiny, red, juicy apple. I am still on a tree waiting to
be picked. Soon I will be at a market ready to be bought and
eaten. Some child will see me there along with other apples,
but I will be the one bought because I am the sweetest and
juiciest one of all! Oh good! Here come some men with ladders
and wooden pails. I feel so excited, I think I have ripened
even more! Here I go along with other apples, but of course
I will manage to get to the top of the pail where the warm
sun will hit me as I go along to the market. Now I'm in the
produce bin, and how wonderful it is! Oh, here comes as a gentle
old lady. She probably wants me for an apple pie. I love to
become apple pies and show off how sweet I am."

Angie (Grade 10)

FLOWER

IMAGERY:

Picture a flower you like(pause)...Note its color... size...shape...fragrance(pause)...Think about this flower and keep it fixed in your mind(pause)...Now look at me (or at some designated spot in the room) with your physical eyes...and while you are looking at me (or at this spot) keep thinking about your flower...See this flower and experience it with your inner eye(pause)...

DISCUSSION:

How many of you could see the flower with your inner eye while looking at me (at the spot) with your physical eye? (Most usually can.) If you have some people who can't at this time, tell them that this skill will become easier with practice. You might even want to lead the group through this activity a second time; however, if you do, change the flower to some other tangible object familiar to them such as a car...book...soft drink... sandwich.

Dear Flower, be ready for the rain to come. Be ready for the bees and the weeds to come. You know you always have to be ready for the rest of your life. I know it's hard being a flower. But you know you are a flower and you are very special to some people like me because I like you, and I will take care of you for the rest of my life.

Adriana (Grade 6)

DESIGNING YOUR OWN IMAGERY JOURNEY
"Yes, You Do Image!"

PREPARATION:

Some people believe they have difficulty visualizing in their mind. To get them started on a successful venture, have them imagine that they are leading a group on an imagery journey. First have them draw what they are seeing...then write it down in the form of a script. Then have them lead the group in the imagery journey as they read it from this script. When this is done, point out that they first had to see this imagery landscape in their mind's eye in order to draw and write it.

MATERIALS:

Crayons, markers, colored pens and drawing paper.

IMAGERY:

Today we are going to prepare ourselves to lead each other on an imagery journey. First think about some beautiful place you would like to take us...a place that will make us feel relaxed...calm...happy (pause)...Now take the colors and draw this place... Don't worry about your art talent...The purpose is to draw this place in whatever way pleases you(pause)... Now write a step by step procedure for leading us; for example..."Take a deep breath and relax...Close your eyes...and imagine you are walking through a beautiful park(pause)...You see wonderful trees...flowers...ferns... and everyone in the park seems very happy...mellow... and they seem to be enjoying the day(pause)...Find a place to sit down and just watch everything that is going on..."

(When this is completed ask for volunteers to actually lead the group on various journeys. Have people display their drawings which served as the basic designs for these journeys.)

This maple leaf is like a friend to me. This leaf sounds like a huge trumpet sounding off for people to notice how lovely the leaf really is. Every leaf is like a breath of fresh air and smells like the mountain-top mist. The maple leaf feels like a new-born baby's skin-so soft and gentle.

Carla (Grade 10)

CENTERING, FOCUSING AND SENSORY EXERCISES

A "warm up" period is often necessary before the mind is still enough to produce and reflect upon inner images. The following exercises calm, center and focus mental activity. We suggest that you begin all imagery activities with one or more of these exercises. You can use these exercises anytime you and/or your people feel the need to relax, center and focus.

Images carry with them certain identifiable feelings, and it is these feelings that help us to better understand the meaning of our images. The sensory-oriented imageries in this section have been designed to help you and your people become sensitive to feeling tones that are visual, auditory, kinesthetic, gustatory and olfactory. Awareness of sensations in the body makes the imagery more vivid, more readily grasped and understood. We recommend that whenever an imagery activity lends itself to multi-sensing, you call attention to multi-sensory processing by asking "What do you see?" "What colors do you sense?" "What sounds do you hear?" "How does this taste?" "What smells are associated with your image?" "How does it feel if you touch it?"

The imageries in this section are arranged sequentially from simple to more complex.

BREATHING

PREPARATION:
Discuss the importance of breathing as a primary factor in relaxation.

IMAGERY:

Close your eyes, and on the count of three take a slow, deep breath, hold it and then exhale with a slight sigh ... Ready ... One ... two ... three ... take a slow...deep breath...hold it...now exhale with a slight sigh(pause)...This time imagine that you are breathing in the freshness of a cool ocean or lake...and as you breathe out you are getting rid of any tiredness, tension or distraction you might be feeling at this time... One...two...three...Take a slow...deep breath...hold it... now exhale with a slight sigh(pause)...Let's do this again... Remember to image yourself breathing in the freshness of a cool ocean or lake...One...two...three...Take a slow ... deep breath...hold it...now exhale with a slight sigh ... ridding yourself of any tiredness, tension or distraction you might be feeling at this time(pause)...Open your eyes... and wiggle your feet and toes...and stretch your arms...hands and fingers(pause)...Stretch your entire body if you need to at this time and feel the gentle relaxation flowing through you(pause)...

BREATHING AND BODY AWARENESS

PREPARATION:

Tell your people that this exercise is similar to "Breathing" only this time they will focus on sensations of relaxation taking place in their body.

IMAGERY:

Close your eyes and on the count of three take a slow... deep breath...Remember to picture yourself breathing in the freshness of a cool ocean or lake...One..two... three...Take a slow...deep breath...hold it...now exhale with a slight sigh(pause)...Let's do this again...One...two...three...Take a slow...deep breath... hold it...now exhale any tiredness, tension or distraction you might be feeling at this time(pause)... Check out your body...what are you feeling now?(pause) ...Some of you may feel a tingling...warmth...vibration ...heaviness in various parts of your body...whatever you are experiencing at this time is fine...Your body is letting go of tension...Let's take another slow...deep breath...One...two...three...Take a slow...deep breath... hold it...now exhale any tiredness, tension or distraction you might be feeling at this time(pause)...Once again check out your body and see what you are feeling(pause)... (Repeat this process as many times as is needed) ... Prepare yourself to open your eyes and return to us here in the room...fully alert...refreshed and ready to work... One...two...three...Take a slow...deep breath...hold it... and as you exhale slowly open your eyes...and wiggle your feet and toes...and stretch your arms...hands and fingers(pause)...Stretch your entire body if you need to at this time and feel the gentle relaxation flowing through you...

DISCUSSION:

Have your people describe their body sensations...what they felt. Some people tend to experience warmth while being relaxed whereas others sometimes experience a chill or lowering of body temperature. Remember to validate all experiences as OK!

CENTERING

PREPARATION:

Discuss the importance of being centered. Mention how we cannot learn while distracted. The purpose of this activity is to provide people with an activity for quieting the mind, getting rid of distractions and focusing attention.

IMAGERY:

Close your eyes and take a slow ...deep breath(pause)... As you exhale, picture a small dot in the center of your forehead(pause)...Now take another slow...deep breath and this time, as you exhale, imagine that you are breathing out through the center of your dot(pause)... Try this again...take another slow...deep breath and as you exhale, breathe out through the center of your dot(pause)...Let's do this once again...Take another slow...deep breath and as you exhale, breathe out through the center of your dot(pause)...Now focus all of your attention on this dot and as you do this, watch your dot get bigger and bigger(pause)...Notice if your dot has color...or many colors(pause)...Now notice if your dot is quiet...still...or is it moving around?(pause)...If your dot is moving around, take another slow...deep breath and tell your dot to slow down with the breath you take(pause)...Now watch your dot become smaller and smaller and smaller until it slowly disappears(pause)...On the count of three, take a slow...deep breath...hold it...and exhale... Feel yourself refreshed...centered...relaxed...alert...

DISCUSSION:

Have your people describe their experience. Remember that whatever they experienced is OK! Ask them to describe what happened to their dot...its color...size...motion. If some were not able to quiet their dots, have them practice taking deep breaths while counting down from ten. With each number, they picture their dot becoming quieter. This usually helps those who are finding it difficult to quiet their minds at a particular time.

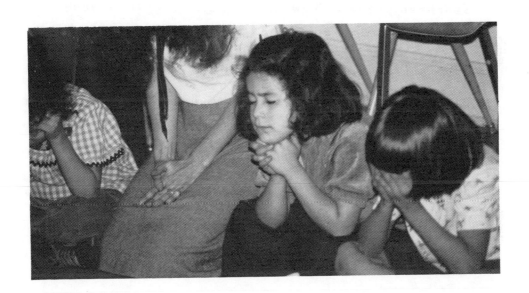

FOCUSING ATTENTION: "Color Circles"

PREPARATION:

Explain that these are "warm up" exercises that calm and focus
the mind, enabling it to clearly see, experience and control
inner images. These should be used anytime you feel distracted
or want to clear your mind.

IMAGERY:

> Picture a red circle in front of you...
> between your eyes ...in the middle of your
> forehead(pause)...Now change the red to green
> (pause)...Now change the green to blue (pause)...
> Now change the blue to yellow(pause)...Now change
> the yellow to brown(pause)... Now make the circle
> any color you wish(pause)... Now put a white dot in
> the center of your circle(pause)...Now change the white
> dot to yellow(pause)...Now remove the yellow dot and
> place a white stripe across your circle(pause)...
> Now change the white stripe to yellow(pause)...
> Now remove the yellow stripe(pause)... What color
> is your circle now?(pause)...On the count of three
> take a deep breath...

VARIATION:

> Picture a green triangle in your mind(pause)...Now change
> it to yellow(pause)...Now to pink(pause)...Now leave the
> color pink but change the shape to a square...Now
> you have a pink square(pause)... Change the pink to blue
> (pause)..Now leave the color but change the shape to a
> rectangle(pause)... Now change the color to purple...

Now you have a purple rectangle(pause)...Now change your purple rectangle into any color or shape you wish(pause)... What shape and color do you have?(pause)...On the count of three...

NOTE:

See NOTE for "Focusing Attention: Lining Up Apples" for suggestions on how to deal with people whose images won't stand still. Be sure to make it okay if some people were not able to get the colors as you named them. The important thing is that they did the exercise and processed the experience with you.

FOCUSING ATTENTION: "Lining Up Apples"

IMAGERY:

Create your mental screen in front of you...
behind your forehead(pause)...and on this screen
picture one apple(pause)...Now picture two apples(pause)
Now picture three apples(pause)...Now picture four
apples(pause)...Now picture five apples(pause)...
Look at them and see if they are all the same color...
...the same shape(pause)...Do they have stems and/or
leaves on them?(pause)...Are they in a row?...in a
circle?...all over your screen?...How are they arranged?
(pause)...Are any of them moving?(pause)...Now open
your eyes and draw what you saw...Be sure to place the
apples just like you saw them on your mental screen.

NOTE:

Some people will see them lined up horizontally whereas
others may see them vertically. Some people arrange them in
various circular and squared patterns. This may tell you how
they line up information in their minds. For example, the
person who lines them up vertically may find it easy to do
math computation where the numbers are arranged vertically
but may have trouble reading sentences that are lined up
horizontally. The person who "can't get the apples to stand
still" may be experiencing momentary mental distraction and
might find it difficult to concentrate at this time. If
this is the case, you can stop and have the person concentrate on slowing the apples down - seeing them becoming
quieter and quieter until finally the apples become still.
Always let your people know that, if their apples continue
to move, it may mean that the person's mind needs to be
quite active on that day. You might try some deep breathing
and centering with the person to see if this helps quiet
the mind. It is important to always let people know that
whatever they experience is OK!

RELAXING THE BODY

PREPARATION:

Discuss the importance of relaxation for focusing attention as well as for both physical and mental well being. You may wish to consult the "Benefits" section of <u>Mind Sight</u>.

IMAGERY:

Close your eyes and take a slow ...deep breath(pause)... Feel the air filling every cell in your body...making you feel lighter and lighter(pause)...Start, now, at the top of your head and picture each cell in your body becoming lighter and lighter...Take another slow...deep breath... and as you exhale you let go of any tension you are hold- ing in your head...around your scalp...in your forehead (pause)...Now continue down your face and neck...Take another slow...deep breath and as you exhale let go of any tension you might be feeling around your face...eyes... cheeks...jaws...neck(pause)...Now take another slow... deep breath and as you exhale let go of any tension you might be feeling in your shoulders...chest...breast... upper back(pause)...Now take another slow...deep breath and as you exhale let go of any tension you might be feeling in your stomach(pause)...And now let go of any tension you might be feeling in your back...Just exhale the tense feeling out of your body and let the good energy around you dissolve the tension for you(pause)... Now take another deep breath and as you exhale let go of any tension you might be feeling in your hips and thighs (pause) ...Continue down your legs, knees, calves, ankles, feet, toes...and let any remaining tension drain out the bottom of your feet into the earth where it is absorbed

79

by the earth's energy(pause)...Now take another slow...
deep breath...and as you do...see yourself filled with a
feeling of lightness...calmness...peacefulness(pause)...
Every cell in your body is thoroughly relaxed(pause)...
On the count of three take another slow...deep breath
and as you exhale...wiggle your hands and feet...become
aware of the sounds and feelings in this room...and when
you are ready...open your eyes and be fully refreshed
and alert...focused and ready to work(pause)...One...
two...three...

VARIATION:

You might wish to lengthen this imagery by including a segment
on light and motion. After the line ending with "calmness...
peacefulness(pause)", add the following:

Imagine that you are floating...floating freely through
the air...Your entire body is flexible...light...and
you are enjoying the feeling of being supported by the
air...If you prefer to create a carpet, cloud or other
support system to help you float then do so at this time
(pause)...Somewhere in your environment find a lovely...
warm sun...and let the sun's rays slowly penetrate through
your skin...making you feel warm...loose...free...The sun
will not burn you(pause)...Take another slow...deep breath
and picture the sunlight giving life to every cell in your
body...giving you a feeling of health...intelligence...
joy(pause)...(Continue with same ending as indicated for
main body of the text.)

DISCUSSION:

Ask your people to describe their experiences. Some may have
felt a tingling sensation. Others may describe having felt
warm, hot or perhaps even cold. Whatever they experienced is
OK!

FLOATING FREE

IMAGERY:

We are going to take an imaginary trip on a beautiful
white cloud...Close your eyes and on the count of three
take a deep breath...One...two...three...Breathe in...
Now breathe out and feel your body becoming very relaxed...Let's take another deep breath...One...two...
three...Breathe in...Now breathe out and feel your
body becoming very relaxed...In your mind see a picture of a beautiful white cloud...very soft...very
strong(pause)...Climb on your cloud and tell it to
take you for a wonderful ride through the sky(pause)
...Look around you and see what's there(pause)...
Can you hear any sounds...or smell anything around
you?...You have one minute of clocktime which is all
the time you need to take the trip on your cloud(pause)
...It's time to come back to our room so tell your
cloud to bring you back here(pause)...Get off your
cloud and thank it for taking you on a wonderful ride
(pause)...On the count of three take a deep breath
...One...two...three...Breathe in...Now breathe out
...Open your eyes...Wiggle your feet and toes...
Stretch your arms and legs...And notice how good you
feel...

DISCUSSION:

Have your people describe their journey on the white cloud.
Where did you go? What did you see? Were you alone? With
others? Do you ever feel like this in real life?

NOTE:

Have them discuss this journey as if they were presently
riding the cloud, i.e., what is it like being on the cloud?
What do you see? How do you feel?

VARIATION:

Have your people become the wind and float freely as the wind.

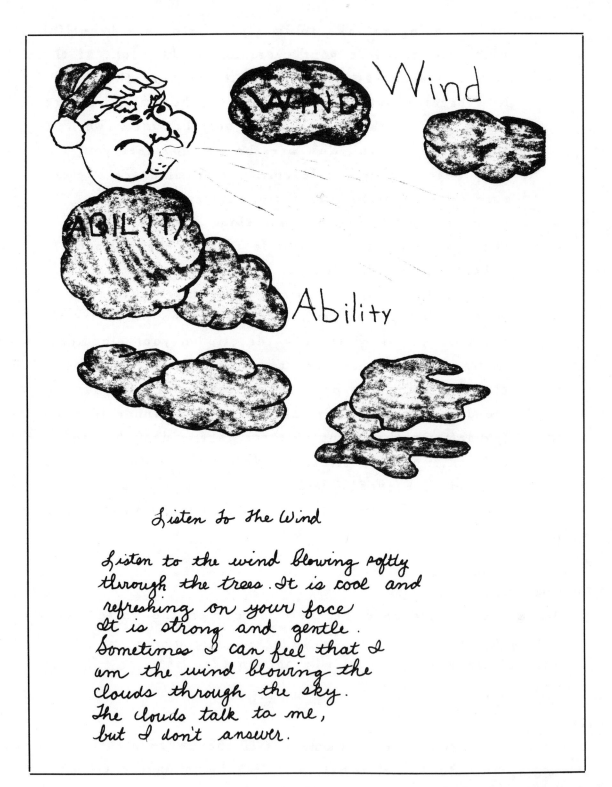

Listen To The Wind

Listen to the wind blowing softly
through the trees. It is cool and
refreshing on your face
It is strong and gentle.
Sometimes I can feel that I
am the wind blowing the
clouds through the sky.
The clouds talk to me,
but I don't answer.

Cindy (Grade 6)

82

FAVORITE PLACE

PREPARATION:

Have your people talk about what senses they ordinarily use
when exploring or learning about something. Do any of them
have a "sixth sense" which they use? In this imagery, they will
practice using each of their senses.

IMAGERY:

Close your eyes...relax...and focus your attention
on your breath...As you gently breathe in...and...
out...in and out...let go of any tensions or concerns
you may have(pause)...Gently float away to a place
that you love to visit...It may be the beach...the
mountains...or home with your family or friends...
Go to any place that you love to be...a place where
you really feel good(pause)...Notice the colors
around you(pause)...the textures(pause)...Notice the
sounds(pause)...and smells(pause)...You may even notice
a particular taste about this place(pause)...Notice how
you feel here...Do you feel happy?...relaxed?...Do the   *Who is with*
sights and sounds please you?(pause)...Now prepare   *you... focus*
yourself to return here to the classroom...When   *on this person...*
I count to three...open your eyes and you'll be   *See them....*
able to write a poem about the place you have visited   *Hear what they*
...remembering the colors...textures...smells...sounds   *say...*
...tastes...and your feelings about this place(pause)   *What are they*
...One...two...three....Open you eyes and begin writing   *doing.....*
your poem. Remember to describe the place in detail...
mentioning each of your senses and indicating your
feelings about being at this special place.

83

SUPPLEMENTARY ACTIVITY:

Art: Have your people do drawings or paintings of the place
and, if you wish, have them print their poems on their
drawings/paintings.

"I close my eyes
And I find myself high in the Sierras
Surrounded by pines, lakes and blue skies
The smells are so clean, so new
The air tastes like cotton candy
I feel strength surging through every vein
I'm glad to be alive."

Ellen (Grade 8)

Watching the sun set...
A flock of seagulls catches my eye
Two palm trees are bent over
           as if asleep.
I am reminded of how late it is
And of how tired I am.

Francisco (Grade 9)

84

SPECIAL PLACE

PREPARATION:

Have your people talk about favorite places they like to visit.

IMAGERY:

> Close your eyes...relax...and focus your attention
> on your breath(pause)...As you gently breathe in...
> and out...in...and out...let go of any tensions
> or concerns you may have...just breathe them away
> (pause)...Now go away to a place that is special to
> you...What is it like?...Is anyone there?...Notice
> what you look like...what you are wearing...
> how you are feeling...Are you younger...older...
> or your same age?...Do you do anything special
> while you are here?...Now take a minute of clock
> time equal to all of the time you need to explore
> this place(pause)...It is time to return to the
> classroom...When I count to three...slowly open
> your eyes...remembering everything you experienced
> in your special place...One...two...three...

ACTIVITY:

Now write a paragraph using the images you experienced.
Remember to describe the place in detail including
nature, animals, buildings, decor, other people and
how you look and feel there. Tell why this place is
special to you.

"I am at the cabin with my family. There are lots of squirrels here waiting for me to feed them. I love being here because I feel safe."

Juan (Kindergarten)

SUPPLEMENTARY ACTIVITIES:

Art: Have your people draw or paint this place.

Poetry: Have them write a poem about it. (You might want them to print the poem on their drawing or painting.)

"Moss and violets line the opening of my cave , and a large oak tree shelters the opening. It is rich and stony within. The darkness gives way as I enter and I see craggy halls of white - bone textured walls of body temperature.

I come to my favorite room in my cave - a grotto like room in which a small waterfall laughs into a tiny pool in the center. This has the feel of being my childhood bedroom, with a bay window and a window seat. It is light and airy. I am welcome here. I love this room best, where I can steal away from the craziness and the inarticulate world cannot smother my clear and shining thoughts.

I can hear the music from my cathedral room down the hall, if I choose, or hear the high majesty of the choir room's singing rocks, blended in lovely music which soars to the top of my cave and leaves as golden tongues of fire into the sky.

The lazy curtains of my bay window are woven of magic white mist,
and no one can see in, although I can see out. The room is mine. No one may enter here unbidden.

Here I am truly safe."

Kathleen (Adult)

87

FAVORITE FOOD

PREPARATION:

Have your people talk about foods they like to eat. Highlight the five senses such as "What does this food smell like? Look like? Feel like? Sound like? Taste like?"

IMAGERY:

Close your eyes and take a slow...deep breath...hold it... now exhale with a slight sigh (Repeat as needed)...Picture your favorite food...and if you have many favorite foods choose one at this time(pause)...Look at this food...see every detail(pause)...Smell it by taking a deep breath and inhaling the good smells from this food(pause)... Now touch the food with your fingers and/or hands and notice the texture...Is it hard...crunchy...soft... silky...thick?(pause)...Now take a bite and notice what happens in your mouth as you do this(pause)... Slowly move the food around in your mouth...What does this feel and taste like?(pause)...What sounds does the food make?(pause)...Now continue eating the food... swallow it...and enjoy each bite you take(pause)... Prepare yourself now to return to us here in the room... fully alert, refreshed and ready to work with this imagery...On the count of three take a slow...deep breath...One...two...three...Take a slow...deep breath ...hold it...now exhale with a slight sigh (pause)... Wiggle your feet and toes...Stretch your arms...hands ... fingers...Stretch your entire body if necessary...

DISCUSSION:

What food did you choose?

Describe the appearance, smell, taste, feel, sound.

Can you still taste it at this time?

Did your mouth water? Or did you have any other body sensations similar to those you experience while actually eating?

88

SYNESTHESIA

PREPARATION:

    Discuss how certain types of music seem to evoke powerful feelings... sensations...sounds...tastes...images and the like. When all senses are evoked simultaneously, we call this "synesthesia". In this activity you will play music that is highly synesthetic and have your people take a multi-sensory trip through the music notes.

SUGGESTED MUSIC:

    "Snowflakes Are Dancing" and "Reverie" from the album <u>Snowflakes</u> <u>are Dancing</u> by Tomita.

IMAGERY:

    In a few moments you will hear a musical selection... and as you do...let your mind wander away from this room and go with the flow of the music...Let the music take you on an inner voyage that will please you... relax you...make you feel good all over...Listen now to the music and let it carry you away(pause)...(Play as much of the selection as you like. For those who have not done much imagery work, two minutes should be enough. For the more experienced, five-ten minutes should be sufficient for them to fully experience the music and sensations.)...As you allow the music to carry you far away ...be aware of where you are...your surroundings...your innermost feelings(pause)...Be aware of sounds...smells... shapes...forms...colors(pause)...Be aware of your feelings as you experience this voyage(pause)...Prepare yourself to complete this multi-sensory voyage and return fully refreshed and ready to work with your experiences(pause)...On the count of three...

SUPPLEMENTARY ACTIVITIES:

    Art: Give your people crayons, colors and/or paints and large pieces of drawing paper. Have them sit in front of this paper. Play the music again, have your people draw their experiences of the music on the sheet of paper. (You might want to have them do this with their eyes closed.)

    Affix large sheets of newsprint to the walls (as gigantic graffiti boards). Have your people take colors and, while listening to the music, draw their feelings and impressions on paper...eyes still closed. Encourage large swooping movements from the shoulder.

    Have them paint the place(s) they visited.

    Poetry: Write a Haiku, Cinquain, etc. describing the experience.

APPRECIATING OUR SENSES: "Sight"

PREPARATION:

Ask if anyone knows a blind person? What do you think it is like to be blind? How would it change your life?

IMAGERY:

Close your eyes and take a deep breath...in...and out...in...and out...and feel yourself becoming more relaxed with every breath you take(pause)...The purpose of our imagery is to help us appreciate our senses. First we are going to experience being blind...Picture yourself as totally blind...you only "see" dark...black in front of you(pause)...You are walking along a street ...Do you have a cane?...guide dog?...friend helping you?...What does this feel like...depending on another to help you know where to go?(pause)...Stop walking now and find a place where you can sit...Listen to the sounds as they pass you by(pause)...Are you able to hear things better now that you can't see?(pause)...Do any of your other senses seem stronger at this time, such as touch, ...smell...taste? ... Now leave this scene and see yourself as having perfect eyesight ... Look at the world around you and see what everything looks like (pause)...On the count of three, take a deep breath and come back to us here in the room...One...two...three... Let's talk about our experiences.

DISCUSSION:

What was it like being blind?
How did you feel inside?
Are those feelings still with you?

Did any of your other senses such as hearing and touch seem stronger? (Some blind people report that they can "feel" what others look like and can "feel" the type of personality the individual has.)

Were there some things you chose not to do because you were blind?

How did you want others to treat you?

SUPPLEMENTARY ACTIVITY:

Have your people role play being blind and share their experiences.

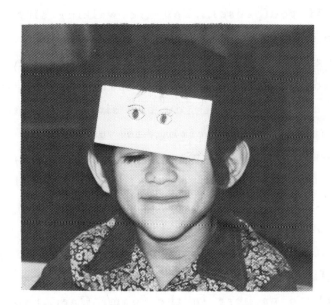

APPRECIATING OUR SENSES: "Hearing"

PREPARATION:

Same as for "Sight" only discuss hearing, and what it would be like to not be able to hear.

IMAGERY:

Repeat the "Sight" imagery beginning with "Close your eyes...and concern from others." Then continue...Now we will experience being deaf...Picture the world as absolutely silent...no sound...only the silence within you(pause)...Do you hear anything within you?...Are you more aware of other senses than you were when you could hear?(pause)...Do you read lips?(pause)...How do you feel while being deaf?(pause)...Are there some things you choose not to do because you are deaf?(pause)... Now leave this scene and...(continue with same ending as for "Sight".)

DISCUSSION:

Same as for "Sight" only substitute vocabulary related to "hearing" and "deafness" wherever appropriate.

SUPPLEMENTARY ACTIVITY:

Have your people role play being deaf and share their experiences.

THE ROSE

PREPARATION:

Tell your people that they will be visiting a garden of roses. Ask them if they have any favorite kinds of roses, favorite colors of roses. Has anyone ever given them a rose? When? On what occasion(s) do they give roses to others? To whom do they usually give roses?

SUGGESTED MUSIC: _Golden Voyage Vol. 1_ by Ron Dexter

IMAGERY:

Close your eyes and on the count of three take a slow... deep breath...(Continue as with "Breathing")...Find a wonderful road and place yourself on this road(pause) ...The day is beautiful and there is much sun...A soft breeze is blowing through the leaves...Enjoy the beauty of the day(pause)...Continue walking down your road until you find a rose garden...There are hundreds of roses in this garden(pause)...Look around until you find one special rose(pause)...You will know this rose because it will stand out among the others(pause)... Examine your rose...look at it carefully...Notice the color...the texture...Feel the stem...the delicate petals ...the thorns(pause)...Smell your rose...Take a deep breath and allow the scent to fill your lungs...to fill every cell in your body(pause)...Silently...within your own mind...tell your rose how beautiful it is(pause)... Now give your rose a voice and let it say something nice to you(pause)...Thank your rose for being there for you and prepare yourself to return to us here in the room...

fully alert...refreshed...and ready to work with the imagery...On the count of three (Continue as with "Breathing")...

DISCUSSION:

Describe your road. Describe the day.

What kinds of roses were in your garden? What colors?

What did your rose look like? Smell like? Feel like?

What did your rose say to you? You say to your rose?

Can you smell the rose even now? Can you still feel it?

SUPPLEMENTARY ACTIVITIES:

Art: Have your people draw and/or paint their garden or their rose.

Poetry: Have them write a poem about the rose.

Writing: Have them write a story about their garden or about their special rose.

Rose

The rose, a simple velvet pattern,
a fiery red diamond,
a silky precious fragrance.
Somehow the priceless flower
becomes a delicate, small princess
being captive and when she breaks
free, she blooms a shiny universe.
The rose - a fiery falling star -
a cloud,
a rainbow,
a fountain,
a golden universe.
The rose - a tiny, playful space.

Kim (Grade 6)

95

Drawing #1 below was drawn by a tenth grade boy without benefit of any imagery experience. The class was simply shown a slide of a rose and given two minutes to draw it, and then another two minutes to write something about their rose. Note how constricted the drawing is, and how reminiscent of rote repetition drills the writing is.

The Rose is very Pretty - The rose is red. The ROSE looks like a nice lady. The Rose is a nice PRESENT FOR A GIRL. The ROSE is EASY TO DRAW ON A SHEET.

Drawing #2 is the work of that same student during the same class period, but now as the result of a guided imagery experience. The students had the same time constraints – two minutes for drawing and two for writing. Note how much more free and unconstricted the drawing is, and note also the significant change in the quality of the writing.

ROSE, you are my BEST FRIEND. YOU ARE MY GIFT FOR MY GIRLFRIEND – AND YOU ARE MY GIFT FOR MY PARENTS AND ALL MY TEACHERS IN SCHOOL. ROSE, you can be THE BEST GIFT A PERSON CAN GIVE TO OTHER PERSONS OR DEAR PARENTS –

CHAPTER SEVEN

GUIDED COGNITIVE IMAGERIES

Imageries that are used for the purpose of teaching basic subjects such as reading, math, science, social studies, geography, language and language arts, as well as physical and psychomotor skills are called <u>cognitive imageries.</u> Cognitive imageries are also used to teach the arts as well as technical subjects such as sewing, home economics, finance, drafting, carpentry and driver's education.

In this chapter we have included those cognitive imageries which have shown themselves to be highly effective in helping people master the skills related to the subjects for which they were used. The imageries are by no means limited to the subject indicated in this chapter. For example, the cognitive imagery entitled "Future World" has been used in social studies classes for presenting concepts related to societies of the future, in geometry and drafting classes for designing houses, cars and cities of the future, in foreign language classes for practicing the future tense of various verbs, and in language arts and writing classes for developing composition skills.

The imageries can be adapted to almost any grade level and/or level of proficiency. It is up to the teacher, counselor, parent, etc. to reword the scripts to fit the readiness level of the individual or group.

We've included visuals of imagery work taken from all age groups who've worked with us. They give you an idea of the uniqueness with which people respond to the imagery activities.

The imageries in this section are arranged thematically, and are not necessarily meant to be used in the order in which they appear.

BEFORE YOU BEGIN, PLEASE REMEMBER TO ...

- ☐ Prepare your people by discussing the importance of using the particular imagery at this time.

- ☐ Check to see if they need any movement types of activities to help settle and center their energy.

- ☐ Check to see if they need a focusing activity to sharpen their inner vision.

- ☐ Make alternate work available in case you have individuals who do not want to do the imagery activity.

- ☐ Prepare any needed materials such as crayons, paints, paper ahead of time.

- ☐ Read the imagery in its entirety and change the wording and pauses to meet the maturity, readiness, interest and proficiency levels of your group.

- ☐ Include a deep breathing/centering exercise to begin the imagery.

- ☐ If the imagery does not include a form for ending the activity (i.e., the "countdown and return to the room"), be sure you have one ready. You can look at the chapter on Getting Started for ideas.

- ☐ Consider adding multi-sensory suggestions such as "What do you see?...hear?...feel?...smell?...taste? ..." whenever you wish to heighten the sensory experience even if they are not included in the actual text of the imagery.

SPELLING,
READING AND
VOCABULARY DEVELOPMENT

SPELLING

PREPARATION:

The idea is to synchronize auditory input with inner imagery. This is done by having people hear the word while forming an inner image of it. Prior to this exercises it is suggested that learners become familiar with the word and its meaning in the context of a personally relevant situation. The following lesson illustrates how we usually present the words. However, teachers vary the presentations according to personal teaching preferences, student needs, learning environment and the like.

Spelling Word: ASTRONAUT

Begin by pronouncing the word and asking if anyone knows anything about an astronaut - who they are, what they do. Show pictures of astronauts. Then have people use the word in a sentence that is meaningful to them; for example, "I read about an astronaut who lives in our state." Then lead your people in the following exercise: Be sure to have the target word (i.e., ASTRONAUT) visible in the room.

IMAGERY:

Look at the board (or overhead, poster, other visual etc.) and see the word ASTRONAUT. Repeat after me A-S-T-R-O-N-A-U-T. (People repeat letter by letter.) Now repeat the entire word ASTRONAUT. (People repeat the entire word.) This time close your eyes and listen to me spell the word. As I do, imagine you are writing each letter on your mind. If you wish, create a screen in front of your closed eyes, behind your forehead, and write the letters there. Take a slow, deep breath... hold your breath...and exhale any tiredness, distraction, or tension you may be feeling(pause)...Do this again... Take a slow deep breath...hold your breath...and exhale any tiredness, distraction or tension you may be feeling

(pause)...(Repeat as needed) Now spell the word ASTRO-
NAUT on your screen...A...S...T...R...O...N...A...U...T.
Open your eyes and check to see if you spelled it
correctly(pause)...Now close your eyes and let's do this
again...Only this time let's spell ASTRONAUT in colors...
A...S...T...R...O...N...A...U...T...Open your eyes and
check to see if you spelled ASTRONAUT correctly(pause)...
Take your pencil (or crayon, paints, markers) and spell
the word ASTRONAUT on your paper...A...S...T...R...O...N...
A...U...T...Close your eyes now and picture the whole word
ASTRONAUT in front of you...Let's spell it out loud...
A...S...T...R...O...N...A...U...T...Whenever you spell
any word, you first need to make a picture of it in
your mind.That will help you to remember it. Anytime
you want to remember how to spell a word, you turn on
this film that you have made in your mind.

VARIATION:

Have people write the word in the air with their fingers or
hands while reading it from their mind screen.

Have them write it on paper, preferably with a crayon or
marker while their eyes are closed and they are reading it
from their mind screen.

Have them write it with their non-dominant hand while reading
it from their mind screen.

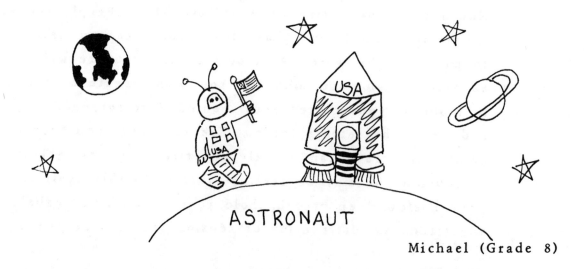

ASTRONAUT

Michael (Grade 8)

SPELLING COMPREHENSION

PREPARATION:

The idea is to have people create a mental picture of what the word means; for example, with the word ASTRONAUT they would picture an astronaut on their screen performing an action such as commanding a space shuttle. The word ASTRONAUT then appears somewhere on or around the picture.

IMAGERY:

Close your eyes...take a slow deep breath...hold it... and exhale any tiredness...distraction...or tension you may be feeling(pause)...(Repeat as needed)...Now on your mind screen make a picture of an ASTRONAUT(pause)... What is the ASTRONAUT doing?(pause)...Is the person in a space shuttle?...on another planet?(pause)...While looking at this picture you will find the word ASTRONAUT written somewhere in this picture...Look for the word now(pause)...If you can't find it then you write the word ASTRONAUT on the picture(pause)...Open your eyes and check the spelling(pause)...Now close your eyes and see the word ASTRONAUT written across your picture(pause)... Now open your eyes and check your spelling once more... (Repeat as needed)...Now take a crayon (marker, pencil) and do a quick sketch of an ASTRONAUT and write the ASTRONAUT on your picture.

NOTE:

When several spelling words have been done in this manner, post the sketches around the room and have people look at them. This enables people to see that although there may only be one way of spelling the word, there are many ways of conceptualizing it.

VOCABULARY DEVELOPMENT/SPELLING

PREPARATION:

Give your people a list of vocabulary words to be learned and spelled. Example:

secretary	accountant	photographer
teacher	gardener	librarian
athlete	dancer	technician

Tell them they will work with a guided imagery exercise to associate specific words with occupations.

NOTE: This activity is also used for presenting oral vocabulary. In this case, you might not want your people to write and spell the words.

IMAGERY:

Close your eyes and picture yourself as a photographer (pause)...What types of pictures would you like to photograph?(pause)...Notice what fun it is to take beautiful pictures(pause)...Now see the word P...H...O...T...O...G... R...A...P...H...E...R...in your mind...and hear the word PHOTOGRAPHER as you write the word PHOTOGRAPHER correctly in your mind. (You might also have them write the word on a piece of paper while their eyes are closed and they are spelling it in their mind.)

NOTE:

Following this exercise have your people look at the word PHOTOGRAPHER, then have them close their eyes and visualize the word. Ask them if the spelling in their mind is the same as the spelling outside of their mind (on the board, overhead, etc.).

SUPPLEMENTARY ACTIVITY:

Art: Have your people use crayons and markers to write the words on paper.

READING COMPREHENSION: "Creating Mental Pictures"

PREPARATION:

The idea is to teach your people ways of forming inner images that are congruent with the words being read and/or listened to. While they are "reading with their eyes" they are simultaneously "forming images in their mind."

Have them close their eyes and listen to you reading a passage. Direct them to create a film in their mind of the story being read. Begin with one sentence at a time. When your people seem able to create inner images of each of these sentences, read an entire paragraph...then several paragraphs combined... and finally, the entire selection. Once your people develop a facility for forming images while hearing words and sentences read aloud, they will do it on their own. The next step is to have them form inner images while they, themselves, are doing the reading.

MATERIALS:

Have crayons, markers and paper available.

IMAGERY: (Excerpted from Albert Camus' <u>The Stranger</u>)

I am going to read the opening passage from Albert Camus, <u>The Stranger</u>. Close your eyes...take a slow deep breath (pause)...exhale any tiredness or distraction you might be feeling(pause)...and prepare yourself to listen carefully to the opening passage... As you listen, create pictures in your mind of what you are hearing...Let your mind create a film of what is being read(pause)...

"Mother died today. Or, maybe yesterday; I can't be sure. The telegram from the home says: "Your Mother passed away. Funeral tomorrow. Deep sympathy." Which leaves the matter doubtful; it could have

105

been yesterday."
Open your eyes and draw what you saw while hearing this
passage. (Give people crayons, colors, and/or markers.)
Show your drawings to each other and tell what
you most remember from the passage. Which aspect(s)
seem most important to you. Which aspect(s) did others
notice that you didn't?

NOTE:

You do not need to require a drawing of each passage.
Do this at least once for every selection - usually
at the end when the entire selection has been read.
At that time you ask people to draw whichever aspect(s)
they most remember and to share these drawings with each
other. We have found that, while looking at each others'
drawings, people note which aspects of the reading they
remembered and which they had not remembered. This
expands comprehension.

Follow the same procedure for individual reading;
however, have your people be aware of the images they
are creating in their minds as they are reading the
words. When they are finished reading, have them stop
and draw their inner images. "Take your books and turn
to page _____. Read the story about _____. As you do,
remember to create pictures in your mind of what you are
reading." Then ask them to verbally share their images.
  Example:
    L: What did you see, hear or feel?
    S: I saw a very lonely, depressed man. I felt sadness
       in my body, and I also felt glad to have friends
       who care for me.

This is how two students pictured "The Mending Wall" by Robert Frost, and their comments about how they feel about fences ...

"It really depends on your neighbor, and how important privacy is to you. I like my privacy, so I'd probably have a fence, even if I lived in the wilderness!"
Michelle (Grade 10)

"I like fences - they give me a sense of security."
Rod (Grade 10)

107

READING COMPREHENSION: "Becoming What We Are Reading"

PREPARATION:

Another way of experiencing the selection is to have people become the characters they are reading. They read the story as if they themselves were in the story.

Example: (The opening paragraph of The Stranger is selected.)

L. As you read the opening passage of The Stranger, imagine you are Meursault receiving the telegram. Check your feelings and responses in the situation. Do you feel sadness? relief? confusion?

SUPPLEMENTARY ACTIVITY:

Have people draw their feelings for each section read; for example, begin by asking people to select a color that represents each of their emotions such as red-anger; yellow-joy; blue-calm. As each section is read they color a segment on their paper to illustrate what they were feeling at the time.

LANGUAGE ARTS
THEMES

DREAM HOUSE

PREPARATION:

Have your people discuss and describe their "Dream House".

MATERIALS:

Colors, crayons and/or charcoals and paper.

IMAGERY:

Close your eyes and let your mind wander to a place
where you find the house of your dreams(pause)...
You decide to create this house of your dreams...
What materials do you need?(pause)...What will the
house look like?(pause)...Notice what environment you
choose...country...city...beach...mountains...(pause)
...Notice the textures of the house...the sounds
around it...the smells...the colors...the shapes...
Spend a minute of clocktime equal to all of the time
you need to create this house(pause)...Now come back
to us here in the room(pause)...Open your eyes...and
draw the house you have created in your mind.

DISCUSSION: (After drawings are completed)
Describe your house to us.
Where is it located?
Describe your surroundings.
Which features of your house do you love the most?
Ask others in the group to tell you which features of your
house they love the most.

VARIATION:

Imagine what your dream house might look like if you lived
in the year 2001.

SUPPLEMENTARY ACTIVITY:

Art: Have your people construct their houses from cardboard, wood, plastic, etc.

Have your people work in groups based on similar concepts of what a "dream house" would look like. Each group builds a "dream house" and these are displayed to the rest of the school, parents, community, etc.

Jane (Grade 8)

112

Joseph Kwon. 23 de octubre.

Vivo en Los Angeles con mi familia. Vivimos
lejos del centro y lejos de aquí. Me gusta vivir
en Los Ángeles. Porque es bonita y tranquila.
No me gusta vivir en Los Ángeles. Porque es
ruidosa. Me gustaría vivir en un Campo
con mi novia.

Gracias...

"I live in Los Angeles with my family. I like living in Los
Angeles when it is beautiful and calm. I don't like to live
in Los Angeles when it is noisy. I would like to live in the
countryside with my sweetheart."

Joseph (Grade 10 - Spanish I)

113

EXPERIENCING THE WORLD THROUGH THE EYES OF A CHILD

PREPARATION:

Same as for "Appreciating Sight", only discuss being very young.

IMAGERY:

Repeat the imagery for "Appreciating Sight" beginning with "Close your eyes...and concern from others." Then continue:
...Now we will experience being a very young child... Picture yourself as very small...one or two years old ...just able to walk and talk a little(pause)...Look around at your world that seems larger and taller to you(pause)...What things look friendly?...Unfriendly? (pause)...Does anything puzzle you?(pause)...How do you feel about the adults around you...Are they nice to you?(pause)...If you feel like talking to people what do you say?(pause)...What do you most want from others around you?(pause)...Now leave this scene and ...(continue with same ending as for "Appreciating Sight")

DISCUSSION:

Same as for "Appreciating Sight" only substitute vocabulary related to "being very young" wherever appropriate.

VARIATION:

Repeat the imagery and this time have your people image what it would be like to be an adult, or someone much older than they are.

LAND OF DREAMS

PREPARATION:

Talk about dreams...what they are...where they come from. Share your own favorite dreams with your people and ask them to tell any dreams they remember.

IMAGERY:

Today we are going to visit the land of dreams.. a very special place where all dreams begin... Close your eyes and take a deep breath...hold it.. now exhale with a slight sigh and let go of any tiredness...tension...or unhappy/sad feelings you might be having right now(pause)...The land of dreams is somewhere up in the sky...so you will need to lift yourself from the earth and travel to the sky... Some of you might create a magic carpet to carry you to the Land of Dreams...or you might create a magic wand...or you might ask some animal or person to take you there...Do whatever you need to get to your Land of Dreams(pause)...Now enter the gate to the Land of Dreams and look around until you find your dream... You will know this dream and it will remember you(pause). Take a good look at your dream and talk to it if you wish...Listen to what it says to you(pause)... Notice if there are any other people...animals... flowers...trees...or other things in your dream... And if there are, just look at them(pause)... Now it is time to leave your Land of Dreams...Say "goodbye" to your dream and return to earth(pause)... On the count of three...

DISCUSSION:

How did you travel to your Land of Dreams?

What did your Land of Dreams look like?

Describe your dream.

If you talked with your dream, what did it say?

Did you learn anything from your dream?

SUPPLEMENTARY ACTIVITIES:

Art: 1)Make a large graffiti board and have everyone draw their dreams on it.

2)Have each person draw their dream, cut it out and hang it as a mobile.

Drama: Select one dream and have others act out the various parts of the dream.

"I saw God in my dream. He was carrying me around the clouds and helping me to have fun jumping on the clouds. There were lots of other kids jumping on the white clouds and one kid was eating a big hamburger with lots of cheese on it! In one corner some other kids were playing Pac Man. Just when everything was getting really exciting my mother came and woke me up!"

Victoria (Grade 2)

NAME CARDS

PREPARATION:

Have your people work in pairs or small groups for this imagery activity. Be sure that they know each other's names. Tell them that in this imagery they will look at each person in the group and see something positive, complimentary and/or appreciative about the person - something that will make them feel good. Before the imagery exercise give each person a large index card or piece of paper, and some crayons or colors to draw and write with. They will use these cards and colors at the end of the imagery exercise.

IMAGERY:

Close your eyes and take a slow...deep breath...hold it ...now exhale with a slight sigh(pause)...(Repeat as needed)...Now picture the people in your group...look at each person one by one...and as you do...let a feeling of appreciation...a compliment...something that will make them feel good about themselves...emerge within you ...This may be a personality trait...a talent...some special gift...a characteristic you're noticing about them...You have one minute of clock time which is all the time you need to look at each person and see something wonderful about them(pause)...Now prepare yourself to come back to us here in the room...fully alert...refreshed...and ready to work with this imagery. ...One...two...three...

DISCUSSION:

Before holding a discussion on what was experienced, have

each person take the colors and write their name in large
letters on the index card. The cards are then passed around
in the small groups and each person writes his/her compliment
on the card of the person whose name appears on the card.

VARIATION:

Have the compliments begin with the letters in the person's
name.

"Tamara is quiet, athletic, musical, tall,
religious and joyful."

Tamara   (Grade 9 - Spanish I)

OCEAN

PREPARATION:

Display pictures and other artifacts from the ocean and have people discuss their experiences at the beach. If possible, play recordings of ocean and beach-type sounds.

SUGGESTED MUSIC:

Environments 1: "Slow Ocean"

IMAGERY:

Travel away to a beautiful beach(pause)...Notice the surroundings...the sand or rocks or grass...trees if there are any...other people if there are other people ...the sky...clouds...winds...waves(pause)...Find a place to lay down your blanket and/or towel...and start walking toward the water...feeling the warmth and mellowness of the day...and as you do this notice how the sand (or rocks...grass) feel beneath your feet(pause)...Now notice the water...the waves...and look around to see if there are any birds flying overhead or walking along the beach(pause)...Can you smell the salty air?...feel the breeze across your face and shoulders?...hear the sounds of the waves crashing on the shore?(pause)...Decide if you want to enter the water and if you do, notice what happens to your body when you dive in the water(pause)... Start swimming around...splashing the water...feeling it cover your head...feel everything...every movement you make in the water(pause)...For those of you who decided not to enter the water, sit down and watch the water... the waves...and any other sights that interest you(pause) ...Now it's time to return to your blanket or towel, so leave the water and begin walking back to where you left your things(pause)...Can you feel the sun on your back...

119

shoulders...face?(pause)...What happens to your feet and legs when you walk across the sand?...Find your blanket and/or towel and sit down on it...and as you do this you realize how thirsty you are...so you look around and find an icy cold drink(pause)...Bring the drink to your lips and take a long cool sip and note all the feelings in your mouth and throat as you do this(pause)...Finish this drink and lay back...close your eyes...and allow your mind to wander off to wherever it wants to go(pause)... Where does your mind go?...Do you recognize the surroundings?...Stay with this for a moment(pause)... Now it's time to return your consciousness to yourself laying there on the blanket or towel(pause)...Become aware of earth beneath your back or stomach...And be aware of the sun and wind and sounds at the beach(pause) ...And now prepare yourself to return to us here in the room, fully refreshed and ready to work with your experiences. On the count of three...

SUPPLEMENTARY ACTIVITIES:

Art: Have people draw and/or paint their experiences.

Poetry: Have people write a brief description or a poem (i.e., Haiku, Cinquain) of their experience.

You can combine both media by having people write their poem on top of their painting or wash.

VARIATION 1:

If you are using this as a science lesson, add items such as sea shells, starfish, sea weed, and any other items included in your science lesson.

VARIATION 2:

Replace "ocean" with "lake" or "river", etc.

"We sat and watched the waves as they came rumbling, rumbling in, and sat and listened to their sound as they went splashing, splashing on. We walked across the gritty land, and left the marks of human man, and listened to the sound of gulls, as they went flying by."
    Chris (Grade 7)

(Note the handwriting change that occurred as Chris got into his poem.)

Grace (Grade 10)

121

PHOTOGRAPHER

IMAGERY:

Picture yourself as a photographer ...You have
a good camera to help you take excellent photographs...
(pause) Your first assignment is to walk around the
school and take pictures of everything that is helpful
to the students...to you...Whenever you find something
that is helpful...stop and photograph it...Take as many
pictures as you want...You have lots of time to do
this...Begin now(pause)...When you have finished,
carefully unload your camera and send the roll of film
to be developed(pause)...A few days later the roll
comes back...you open the envelope and look at your
pictures...What did you photograph?...Which pictures
came out best?(pause)...Now take your best photographs
and pin them up on a bulletin board that says "Helpful
Things Around The School"...You will notice some photos
taken by other people too!...Look at these!...Are there
any like yours?...Now on the count of three...

DISCUSSION:

Have your people discuss the questions posed in the
imagery activity.

SUPPLEMENTARY ACTIVITY:

Art: Have your people make pictures of the items they
"photographed".

VARIATION 1:

Repeat exercise for "not-so-helpful" things around
the school.

VARIATION 2:

Repeat exercise for "helpful/not-so-helpful" things around home, neighborhood, city, country.

"The most serious problem at my school is smoking."

Carlos (Grade 9 - French I)

VARIATION 3:

Have students travel to another planet and photograph what they see.

VARIATION 4:

Have the students "walk through their school day", taking photographs of each class they take, and then verbalize how they feel in each of their classes.

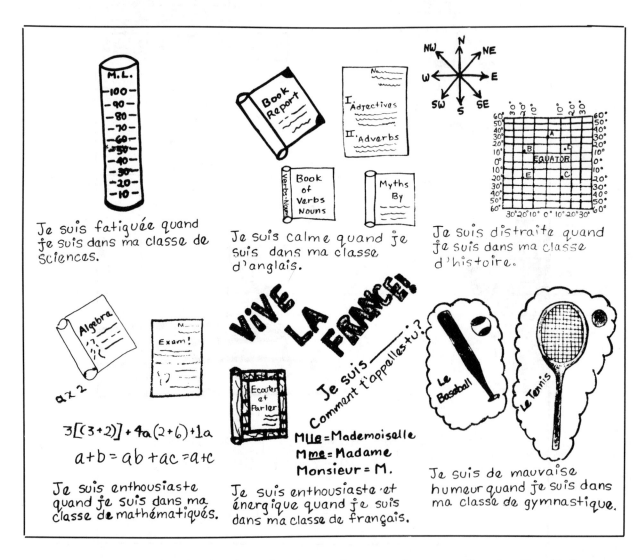

"I am tired when I am in my science class, calm in English class, distracted in history class, enthusiastic in math class, enthusiastic and energetic in French class, and in a bad mood in gym class."

Kim   (Grade 10 - French I)

PICNIC AT THE BEACH

PREPARATION:

Display pictures and other material on food and beverages that make up a delicious picnic scene.

SUGGESTED MUSIC:

Environments 1: "Slow Ocean"

IMAGERY:

Begin in the same manner as for OCEAN. Ending with the line "What happens to your feet and legs when you walk across the sand?" Then continue in the following manner:

Suddenly you smell a delicious beach barbecue ... hot dogs...hamburgers...charcoals glowing in the fire ... and you look around and see a group of people having a picnic on the beach(pause)...You walk toward them, and are aware of everything that they have prepared for the picnic...What do you see?(pause)...These people notice you looking at them and they invite you to join them. You say you would like this very much. What do they offer you to eat and drink?(pause)...You start talking with these people about yourself...your interests... and they talk with you about theirs. What do you say to them? What do they say to you?(pause)...Suddenly you realize it's time to go so you thank them for the food and conversation and slowly walk back to your own blanket...filled with the good feelings of a beautiful day spent with some very nice people. Pick up your towel and walk away from the beach ... and prepare yourself to return to us here in the room, fully refreshed and ready to work with your experiences. (Pause)...On the count of three...

125

DISCUSSION:

Describe the groups of people whom you met.

What were they eating? Drinking?

What did you tell them about yourself?

What did they tell you about themselves?

What did you most like about this experience?

SUPPLEMENTARY ACTIVITIES:

Art: Have people draw and paint their experiences.

Poetry: Have people write a brief description or a poem (i.e., Haiku, Cinquain) of their experience.

VARIATION:

Replace "beach" with "lake" or "river".

La Plage

La plage est tres chaude. Je suis à la plage pendant les vacances avec mes amies et ma soeur. Je me sens heureuse à la plage mes amies y sont heureuses. Nous jouons et écoutons la radio. Nous aimons la plage.

"The beach is very hot. It's vacation and I am here with my friends and my sister. I feel happy at the beach and my friends are happy there. We're playing and listening to the radio. We like the beach."

Michelle (Grade 9 - French I)

TREE

PREPARATION:

Discuss the idea that we can't really know another person unless we can somehow experience the person's world as they experience it. The same is true for flowers, plants, trees, animals, stars, planets, body cells, rocks, clouds, colors, and the like. So we project ourselves into a person or thing, becoming them (or it) in our body, while experiencing them (or it) in our minds and with our emotions.

IMAGERY:

Picture a tree in front of you(pause)...Examine your tree very carefully...Is it tall or short(pause)... Are there many branches or only a few?(pause)...What do the leaves look like?...Are they small or large? ...long?...slender?...pointed?(pause)...What about the trunk? Is it smooth?...or rough?...fat?...or skinny?(pause)...What color is the trunk?...dark brown?...light brown?...white?...Or does your trunk have many different colors?(pause)...Now project yourself into your tree(pause)...Notice what you are feeling at this time(pause)...All of a sudden, a gentle breeze begins to blow through your leaves... your branches...what does this feel like?(pause) ... The sun is shining on your leaves...What does this feel like?(pause)...Now listen to the other sounds around you...With the ears of a tree what do you hear?(pause)...Now look around you and with the eyes of a tree, what do you see?(pause)...It is time now to let go of being a tree...Take a deep breath and as you exhale become your human self once more(pause)...Do you notice any changes in your feelings as you switch from being a tree to being a

127

human person(pause)...Now be fully yourself and as yourself take one more look at your tree...In your mind thank your tree for cooperating with you in this experience(pause)...Now slowly walk away from your tree and continue walking until you once again enter our room(pause)...When you arrive here be fully aware of the sounds in this room...the feeling of the chair(floor, rug, etc.)...On the count of three take a deep breath...

DISCUSSION:

What kind of tree was in your imagery? Describe it.

What did it feel like to be this tree?

What did you a)most like b) least like?

How is the tree like you? (i.e., tall, short, deeply rooted, reaching for the sky, easy to climb, fun and helpful to be with?)

What changes in your body and emotions and thoughts did you notice while changing from being a tree to being a human?

SUPPLEMENTARY ACTIVITY:

Art: Have people draw their tree and show how they and their tree are alike.

EXAMPLE:

"My tree is deeply rooted in the earth and so am I. I'm a very earthy person."

VARIATION:

Be a flower, grass, a stone, a wave, a rock, a cloud, etc.

The Secret of the Grass

The grass seems to cry because it is wet.
I think I know why it cries. It's because
it is too cold and people walk on it.
But when it's day, it seems like the
grass is soft little pillows and it's roots
grow and grow just like people do. It's
friends are dirt and little tiny bugs,
with nature's love.

Man Phan (Grade 6)

Stone

I am a stone
A jagged one
Down below the Rockies.
They throw me
In the water.
The waves push.
I get smaller smaller, smaller
Now a grain of sand.
Children making sand castles
I get caught
On their hands
Travel
To a far off land
Never to be seen
Again.

Gina (Grade 6)

129

VACATION MEMORIES
(Beating the Day Back Blues)

PREPARATION:

This imagery is designed to help you and your people recapture
the most memorable moments of vacation. You might want to
start by asking people to talk about where they went, what
the weather was like, what they did, with whom they spent
their vacation, what special things happened. Then lead them
in the imagery activity. On the other hand, you might begin
by telling them that you will lead them in an imagery activity
to help them recapture favorite moments during their vacation,
and that a discussion will follow the imagery experience. We
have found both ways to be satisfactory.

IMAGERY:

Close your eyes and take a slow...deep breath...hold it
...now exhale with a slight sigh(pause)...(Repeat as
needed)... Travel back to a favorite time during your
vacation...a time that seems very important to you(pause)
When you arrive there...look around and notice everything
in the environment(pause)...Listen to the sounds(pause)
...Notice any smells(pause)...Touch some things(pause)
...If possible taste something there(pause)...Are you
alone or are you with others?(pause)...What's happening
at this time during your vacation?...You have one minute
of clock time which is all the time you need to
experience a special time during your vacation(pause)...
Prepare yourself to come back to us here in the room...
fully alert and ready to work with this imagery...On the
count of three ...

[handwritten margin notes: Who is there with you / See them doing / What are they doing / Someone speaks to you... / How do you / Answer.]

130

DISCUSSION:

Have people talk about their vacations. Use the questions in the imagery as a guide.

SUPPLEMENTARY ACTIVITIES:

Art: Have your people draw or make murals of their vacations, focusing on favorite moments, favorite people, favorite foods, and the like.

Writing: Have them write compositions on their vacations.

NOTE: After everyone has written a short composition, select a few at random, read them aloud, and have the others guess which person belongs to each of the vacation stories being read.

VARIATION:

Have your people take an "imaginary" vacation imagery journey.

"During vacation, I dance once in a while, I relax with my family, I swim in the ocean, and I yell "Hey, Roberto!" with my friends."

Socorro (Grade 10 - Spanish I)

"I'm going to take a trip to Denmark. I'm leaving for this trip tomorrow, and I'm going alone. I'm taking a plane and I feel very excited! I'm taking two suitcases with me, lots of money and my passport. As soon as I arrive there, I see many pretty girls! I buy souvenirs. I go out with pretty girls to visit those points of interest, and I get married! I stay in Denmark for two years. I come back in the Love Boat!"

Richard (Grade 10 - French I)

SOCIAL STUDIES

ABRAHAM LINCOLN
(Learning About Important People)

PREPARATION:

Discuss the personal and professional qualities of the
person targeted in this lesson. For example, suppose you
are talking about Abraham Lincoln and his contributions
as president. Begin with some guide questions and background information about Mr. Lincoln. If possible show
pictures of the president and other visuals that illustrate his early life as a child and adolescent, and his
political career as well. Be sure to include information on the social/political situation in the United
States at the time of his election.

IMAGERY:

Picture yourself as Abraham Lincoln...sixteenth president
of the United States(pause)...You have just been elected
President and you are in the process of delivering your
first presidential speech to the nation(pause)...Look out
at the people...How many are there?...What are they
wearing?...Are they friendly toward you?(pause)...
You begin talking to them...giving them your promises...
sharing with them your hopes for the country...asking
them to help you...Listen to what you say(pause)...As
you are speaking how are the people responding?...Do they
think you are sincere?...Are you being honest with
them?...Are you telling them the truth?(pause)...Now
end your speech and see how the people respond. Do
they applaud? Boo?...Ask questions?(pause)...Complete
this experience and prepare yourself to return to us
here in the room(pause)...On the count of three, take
a deep breath...

DISCUSSION:

Have your people discuss the questions posed in the imagery activity.

SUPPLEMENTARY ACTIVITY:

Writing: Have your people rewrite their speech in the first person as if they were Mr. Lincoln.

VARIATION:

Use this projection activity for having your people identify with any person they are studying such as Washington, Kennedy, famous writers, politicians, athletes, artists, etc...

Kristopher (Kindergarten)

136

DISCOVERING OUR ROOTS

PREPARATION:

Have your people share ideas about their ancestors, where they lived, how they lived, their nationality, profession, special talents, influence on your family.

IMAGERY:

Let us breathe deeply together...in...and out... in...and out...As you continue to breathe allow the muscles in your body to become very relaxed(pause)... Now let all concerns go...breathe them out...feel the peace within you(pause)...Imagine that you are moving back in time and space to where your ancestors live... Notice the environment in which they live(pause)...What are they doing?...They may be hunting...farming... building...cooking...singing...dancing...creating art... climbing...taking care of animals...Whatever they are doing, watch closely so that you will be able to remember every detail about them(pause)...What do you notice about their appearance?(pause)...What do you notice about their family life?(pause)...What types of animals are present?(pause)...What are the colors...smells...and sounds that you are aware of?(pause)...Now, pick out one particular ancestor from the group...Look at him or her closely...Notice the age...dress...and facial expression (pause)...Now follow him/her as s/he goes about daily activities...You have a minute of clocktime equal to all the time that you need to learn all you can about this ancestor(pause)...Now become aware of your body as you sit here in the classroom...When I count to 10...open your eyes and write about your ancestors in general... then describe the one ancestor in particular...Remember to include all of the colors...smells...and sounds... as well as your feelings about your ancestor.

DISCUSSION:

Describe your ancestors and the one in particular.

What were your ancestors doing?

Have you and your family continued any of the customs of your ancestors?

What makes your one ancestor so special?

SUPPLEMENTARY ACTIVITY:

Art: Make a mural of these ancestors. Cut out the ancestors and make a mobile.

VARIATION:

Create an imagery tracing the family tree. Stress the immediate family, and what the person most likes about his/her parents and brothers or sisters.

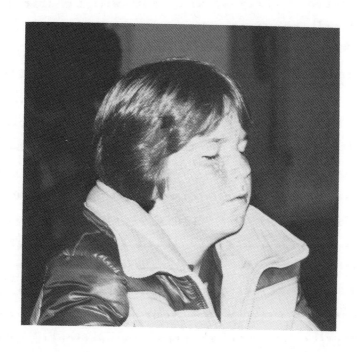

138

"My ancestors lived on the Indian reservation in Montana. Life was very hard for them because they did not have modern conveniences like we enjoy today. They hunted animals to provide food and clothing and also used the hides to build their homes. I love to sit in front of the fireplace and listen to my father speak of my great-grandfather who was the medicine man of his tribe. I close my eyes and picture myself living in those days. I usually find myself wishing I lived then instead of now, because people then lived much more in harmony with the earth and did not get so caught up in material belongings which don't matter when you go to die. Our family now is not very rich, and sometimes I find it hard to come to school and get teased about my clothes. It helped me to think back to what life was like for my ancestors, because I realized my life now is very easy compared to the difficulties they faced, and if they could still be happy, so can I."

Laura (Grade 9)

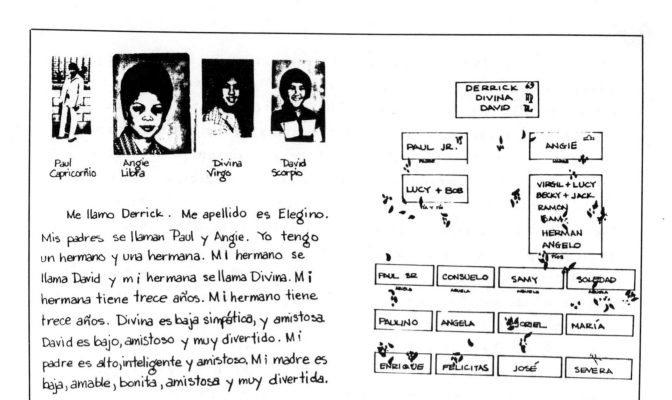

Me llamo Derrick. Me apellido es Elegino. Mis padres se llaman Paul y Angie. Yo tengo un hermano y una hermana. Mi hermano se llama David y mi hermana se llama Divina. Mi hermana tiene trece años. Mi hermano tiene trece años. Divina es baja simpática, y amistosa. David es bajo, amistoso y muy divertido. Mi padre es alto, inteligente y amistoso. Mi madre es baja, amable, bonita, amistosa y muy divertida.

"I'm Derrick. My last name is Elegino. My parents are Paul and Angie. I have one brother and one sister. My brother is named David and my sister is named Divina. My sister and brother are thirteen years old. Divina is short, nice and friendly. David is short, friendly and funny. My father is tall, intelligent and friendly. My mother is short, loving, pretty, friendly and funny."

Derrick (Grade 9 – Spanish I)

EXPLORING OTHER COUNTRIES: JAPAN

PREPARATION:

Have your people discuss cultural aspects of Japan such as language, education, foods, athletics, politics, geography and the like. If possible show visuals of the country. (Follow the same procedure for any country you wish to explore.)

IMAGERY:

Close your eyes and imagine that you are traveling through space and time to Japan...When you arrive there you notice all of the vibrant colors...You notice everything about the environment...the houses ...the types of transportation...what people do (pause)...You meet a friend who takes you home and prepares a meal for you...You enjoy the smells and the tastes of Japanese food(pause)...Your friend introduces you to his/her family and friends and shows you what sports he or she plays...You listen very carefully to the language spoken in Japan and to the songs the people sing(pause)...You spend a day with your friend at school noticing everything about school life in Japan(pause)...You then find yourself traveling back through space and time and arriving here in the classroom...When I count to three...slowly open your eyes...remembering all the details...colors...tastes ...sounds...and smells of life in Japan...One...two ...three...Write down what you remember from this experience.

DISCUSSION:

Describe Japan in detail - people, language, shops, food, family life, hobbies, etc.

In what ways is Japan like America? How is it different?

If you were to live in Japan for any length of time, how would your life be different from how you now live?

SUPPLEMENTARY ACTIVITIES:

Art: Have people draw six major aspects of life in the particular country of study, i.e., crops, dress, sports, education, architecture, entertainment.

Drama: Have your people describe themselves as if they were Japanese. They speak in the first person.

Music: Play music appropriate to the country being studied.

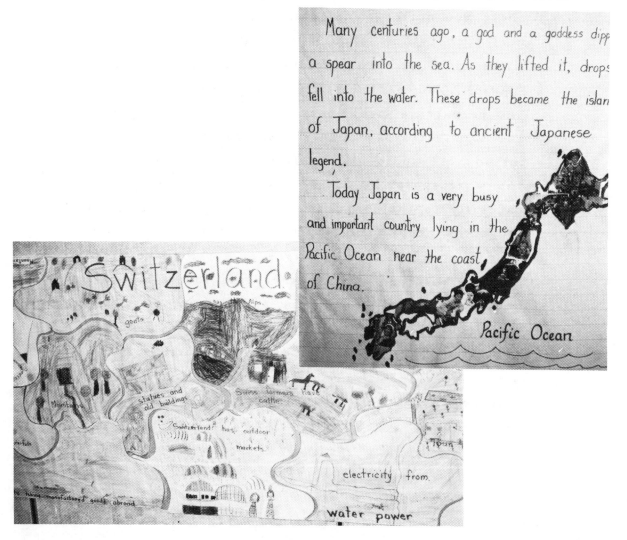

FUTURE WORLD

PREPARATION:

Have students discuss future possibilities; i.e.,what the
world will be like 100, 500, 1000 years from now. Emphasize
body shape, clothes, housing, transportation, work/jobs,
cities, recreation, leisure time activities and the like.

IMAGERY:

Travel now 100 years in the future...You
are completely free of all influences from this
year...this time...this date(pause)...Now look
around you and note what you see(pause)...Look
at bodies...body shapes...What do people
look like?(pause)...Now look at the clothes(pause)...
now look at housing...where people live(pause)...
What kind of transportation do people have?...
Are there cars?...planes?...boats?(pause)...What
kind of work do people do?...What kinds of jobs are
available?(pause)...What do cities look like?(pause)...
schools?(pause)...hospitals?(pause)...grocery stores?
(pause)...Other stores?(pause)...Are there telephones?
(pause)...televisions?(pause)...stereos?(pause)...
Is mail delivered to each home?(pause)...
(Repeat procedure for 500...1,000 years...) On the
count of three...

DISCUSSION:

Have your people discuss the questions posed in the imagery
activity.

SUPPLEMENTARY ACTIVITIES:

Art: Have people draw their visions of the future.

Have people make models of (or design) future cars, homes, clothes, etc.

Drama: Have people make up a future language and converse with each other in this language.

VARIATION:

Have your people explore just one aspect of this future world such as..."schools in the future"..."people of the future".

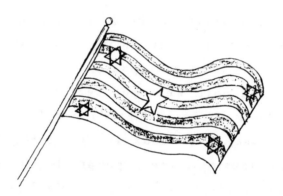

"Behold the flag of the united planet Utopia, which no mortal man has ever set eyes on. We come in peace from a distant galaxy to help you. We have stopped all disease and war no longer worries us. We come to help you rid this planet of disease and to unite all the peoples of the earth under a single leadership. We know that there are some among you who don't think we can accomplish this, but we have done so in our galaxy and we can do it here on earth as well. It will take time, and once it is accomplished we will return to our planet of Utopia and leave you. We will continue to watch you develop and send help whenever you ask for it. We hope you won't mess things up once we get things right down here, because we really like our galaxy better and we'd rather not have to come back and do it all over again!"

Francisco (Grade 10)

144

OTHER LANDS - OTHER CULTURES

IMAGERY: (Using France as the country being studied)

You have just landed at Charles de Gaulle Airport
outside of Paris...You leave the plane and enter
the airport...Everyone around you is speaking
French...You arrive at the customs desk where
a neatly uniformed officer hands.you a card to
fill out...This card tells the customs agent if
you have anything to declare...Does the person
speak French or English to you?(pause)...After
you leave the airport, you take a taxi to your
hotel on the left bank...On the way, the driver
takes you past the Seine...You see it winding
through Paris, framed by buildings older and
more decorative than any you've seen in America
(pause)...You also pass several outside cafes
on your way(pause)...Finally you arrive at
your hotel and you pay the taxi driver...How
much do you pay?(pause)...Now enter your hotel
and walk up to the concierge and give him/her
your name(pause)...Does this person speak English
or French to you? What does he/she say?(pause)...
You sign in and go up to your room...What does
it look like?(pause)...What do you see when you
look out the window?(pause)...It's time for you
to return from this trip now, and return to us
here in the room(pause)...On the count of three...

DISCUSSION:

Have your people discuss the questions posed in the imagery
activity.

PAST HISTORY

PREPARATION:

Tell your people that in this activity they will explore
a place in time and space that they have never visited
before. They will go backwards in time. They will act as
a journalist who has come to learn as much as possible about
this undiscovered place. Tell them to pay attention to all of
the colors, sounds, smells and feelings that they experience
on this trip.

IMAGERY:

Close your eyes...Follow your breath in and out of
your nostrils...and as you follow your breath...you
will notice that you are becoming very relaxed...yet
mentally alert(pause)...Now let go of any thoughts or
expectations you may have...and allow yourself
to let your imagination and your mind float free
(pause)...Imagine that you are walking outside this
classroom...outside this school...and you find a
time machine in front of the school...Walk
around the time machine...noticing its shape and
controls(pause)...You climb into the time machine
and set the controls for a time in history many
years past(pause)...As soon as the controls are set
to the time in history that you wish to visit...you
feel yourself being gently yet swiftly lifted up and
transported to the time you have chosen(pause)...
When you have landed you begin to explore this
new land...You notice the environment...the life
forms...interesting creatures...You notice the people
and you try to communicate with them and find out

about their culture...their family life...what they
eat and how they live(pause)...If they have music...
you will be able to bring back a song from their
world(pause)...Notice their art(pause)...You may
wish to find a particular person or creature and to
spend some time with this being...You have one minute
of clocktime which is all you need to carry out your
explorations in this world(pause)...It is now time for
you to leave this world and climb back into the time
machine...You may wish to tell the people (creatures,
you have befriended) that you will return another time
(pause)...Set the dials in the time machine to this year
and return safely here to the classroom(pause)...On the
count of three, take a deep breath, and return to us
here in the room, fully alert and refreshed and ready
to work with your images...One...two...three...

SUPPLEMENTARY ACTIVITY:

Art: Have your people do drawings or paintings of this place.

VARIATION:

Designate a specific era such as 1492 or the "17th Century"
for your people to visit.

"I saw the year 1001. People rode on horses and men
wore clothes made of silks, satins and ruffles. I'm
glad I didn't live then, because I would have hated
that! People lived in huge stone houses and cooked
their food in fireplaces. The music was funny sounding
stuff - nothing like the Beach Boys or any of the other
good groups we have today. They didn't have stereos or
tape recorders to play their music on either. I met a
man who worked for the government, and he wrote books
by hand because people didn't have typewriters. He let
me spend the day with him. We rode around in a carriage
and talked to lots of other men about boring things
that governments take care of."

Darryl (Grade 9)

148

MATHEMATICS

ANGLES

PREPARATION:

Teach your people procedures for constructing various angles and/or shapes. If possible, have them build the shapes from cardboard, string or yarn.

IMAGERY:

Imagine yourself to be inside the shape you have constructed(pause)...Travel from angle A...then to angle B...then to angle C...then to angle D...Do all the angles seem to have the same amount of space?...Are they the same size?(pause)...Stand in the center of the shape...What do you see when you look around?(pause)...Finish doing this, and prepare yourself to return fully refreshed to work with this imagery(pause)...On the count of three...

DISCUSSION:

Have your people discuss the questions posed in the imagery activity.

VARIATION:

Pose various situations to your students representing real-life concerns over which they might be in conflict with others (i.e., parents, friends, etc.). Have them construct angles which represent their degree of openness in talking about each of these situations with these people.

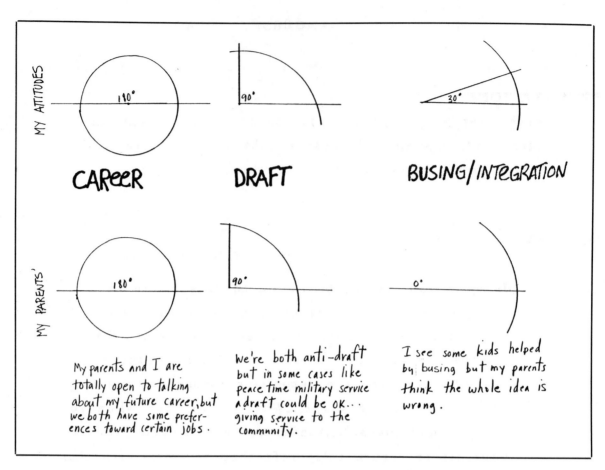

MY ATTITUDES

| CAREER | DRAFT | BUSING/INTEGRATION |

110°

90°

30°

MY PARENTS'

180°

90°

0°

My parents and I are totally open to talking about my future career, but we both have some preferences toward certain jobs.

We're both anti-draft but in some cases like peace time military service a draft could be OK... giving service to the community.

I see some kids helped by busing but my parents think the whole idea is wrong.

Sharon (Grade 10)

152

CONCEPT FORMATION

PREPARATION:

If you are working with younger children, teach concepts related to grouping similar items before doing this imagery.

IMAGERY:

Repeat the imagery titled "Lining Up Apples" and have your people do drawings of what they experienced.

Then have them hold up their drawings for the others to see and note which ones seem similar in terms of how apples are lined up; i.e., vertically, horizontally, in a circle. Then ask people to walk around and find others whose drawings are similar and form "similarity groups" with these people. Then ask each group to tell the class how they see their drawings as similar.
EXAMPLE:

"Everyone in our group had 2 green and 3 red apples placed in a circle." "We all had red apples arranged in a straight line going across the page."

VARIATION:

After suggesting that the drawings be compared according to line up, you might want to vary the criterion to include color combinations, size of apples, shapes, blemishes, etc. This will enable the students to see that there are many valid criteria for forming clusters, and once the criteria are changed, objects can become members of different clusters.

EQUATIONS

PREPARATION:

Tell your people that you will lead them in a guided imagery that will help them to understand equations. You might prefer to teach equations prior to this imagery, thus using the imagery as a means for reinforcing information, or you may prefer to begin the lesson with this imagery and then go into your explanation of equations. We have found that by beginning the lesson with the imagery and then teaching the math concepts, our people tend to learn the concepts more quickly.

IMAGERY:

Close your eyes and take a slow...deep breath... hold it...now exhale with a slight sigh(pause)... (Repeat as needed)...Imagine yourself having a won- derful vacation...everything is perfect...See what you are doing and how you are feeling(pause)...Where are you?(pause)...Are you alone or with others?(pause) ...What's going on?(pause)...What is the scenery like? (pause)...What makes you so happy on this vacation? (pause)...What things or people or situations are missing that, if they were there, might spoil your vacation?(pause)...Is there one thing in particular that makes this vacation so special?(pause)...Now prepare yourself to come back to us here in the room... fully alert...refreshed...and ready to work with this imagery...On the count of three...

DISCUSSION:

Have your people describe their perfect vacations. Use the questions in the imagery as a guide. When this is completed, then provide them with a basic equation such a + b = c, where c = a perfect vacation. Then have them fill in their ingredients for a perfect vacation. Once they've mastered this idea you can make the equation more complex such as a + b - c = d, where d = a perfect vacation.

EXAMPLE:

Lots of sun + good friends - school work =
a perfect vacation.

SUPPLEMENTARY ACTIVITIES:

Art: Give your people small sheets of paper or index cards and have them draw their ingredients. Then cut these out and make equation mobiles.

Give each person small index cards and have them draw one ingredient on each card. Then place all the drawings in one pile and have people go through the pile and select various ingredients for a perfect vacation. Then they place these in an equation.

EXAMPLE:

Person selects pictures of a beach, a bottle of coke, a surfboard, rain, days of the week and money, then arranges the pictures as follows:

$$\frac{(\text{beach} + \text{bottle of coke} + \text{surfboard} - \text{rain}) \times \text{money}}{\text{days of the week}}$$

= a perfect vacation

VARIATION:

Use other math. operations such as division and multiplication (see example above) squares and square roots, etc, to create more elaborate equations.

GEOMETRIC SHAPES: SQUARE, RECTANGLE, RHOMBUS, TRAPEZOID

PREPARATION:

After your people have studied the definitions for the shapes presented in the lesson, have them draw each shape and write out its definition. Then tell them they are going to create a "futuristic city" from the shapes that they have studied.

IMAGERY:

Travel away 1,000 years into the future(pause)...All of the buildings, cars, sidewalks, roads are made from the geometric shapes you've just studied...Examine these things very closely and imprint them on your mind(pause)...Which building shapes please you the most?...In doing this are you discovering new architectural possibilities?(pause)...Finish this now(pause) ...On the count of three.

DISCUSSION:

Draw what you saw and label each shape.
Have your people draw their cities and label each shape. They then show their drawings to each other and discuss the shapes.

VARIATION:

Have your people use various geometric shapes to draw a person.

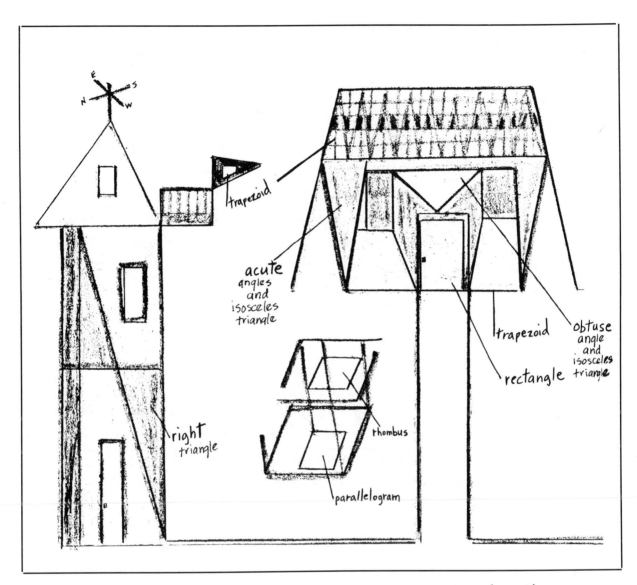

The labels in the drawing:

trapezoid

acute angles and isosceles triangle

right triangle

parallelogram

rhombus

trapezoid

rectangle

obtuse angle and isosceles triangle

Susan (Grade 10)

157

MATH COMPUTATION

PREPARATION:

The idea is to simultaneously match auditory input with inner imagery. This is done by having people hear numbers and various mathematical operations while picturing the numbers and operations in their mind. Prior to this imagery activity, it is suggested that learners become familiar with the basic math concepts being presented and have a thorough understanding of the terms being used such as addition, subtraction, multiplication, division, etc.

Math Operation: Two plus three equals five.

$$\begin{array}{r} 2 \\ + 3 \\ \hline 5 \end{array}$$

Begin by having your people watch the entire operation on the board, overhead, etc. Then have them repeat the process 2 + 3 = 5 out loud with you. Following this have them close their eyes and imagine the procedure in their mind while you repeat it aloud ...

IMAGERY:

Close your eyes...take a slow deep breath...hold it... and exhale any tiredness...distraction...or tension you may be feeling(pause)...(Repeat as needed)...Now on your mind screen picture a two...If you like, you might want to color it red...yellow...or whatever color pleases you(pause)...Now under your two, make a three appear...and if you like, color your three(pause)... On the left of your three make an addition sign... and color the sign(pause)...Now under the three draw a straight line and color the line(pause)...Under the line make a five and color it(pause)...Now look at the whole operation...Two plus three make five(pause)... Open your eyes and check to see if your images are the same as those on the board (in the book, etc.) (pause)...Now close your eyes and again make a picture of two plus three equals five(pause)...(Repeat as needed) ...Now open your eyes and take your pencil (crayon, marker, etc.) and draw this operation on your paper... You might want to use the exact colors you saw...

VARIATION 1:

When calling out the numbers, direct your people to see the numbers in a specific color such as "See a red two (pause) ... and underneath your red two see an orange three (pause) ... On the left of your orange three, make a yellow addition sign (pause)...Underneath the orange three, make a brown line (pause)...Underneath your brown line, make a green five." (pause)...

VARIATION 2:

Have people write the numbers in the air with their fingers or hands while listening to you read the operation and simultaneously visualizing it in their mind.

VARIATION 3:

Repeat the procedure for multiplication, division, squaring, finding square root, etc.

SCIENCE

ATOMS

PREPARATION:

Discuss ideas related to atoms and atomic structure;i.e. electrons, protons, neutrons, energy waves.

IMAGERY:

Imagine yourself becoming small...microscopic in size...so small that you can only be seen by a powerful electron microscope.(pause)...Now imagine that an atom is in front of you...Using all of your powers of concentration, you now enter the atom...Look around and examine the atom in detail...What do you see?(pause)... What do you feel?(Pause)...Do you hear anything? ...If so, what?(pause)...Are there any smells? (pause)...Does what you are observing remind you of anything you have ever seen or experienced before? (pause)...Prepare yourself now to come back to us in the room...fully refreshed...awake... and ready to share your experiences(pause)...On the count of three take a deep breath...

DISCUSSION:

What did it feel like being microscopic in size? What body sensations accompanied these feelings?
Describe your atom in detail.

SUPPLEMENTARY ACTIVITY:

Art: Have your people draw and label their atom.

CREATING A HELPFUL MACHINE

PREPARATION:

Have your people think about types of machines that could be helpful to them at this time. Use the opening sentence "I would like a machine that..." Tell them to answer this statement in their own mind, but not aloud to the others. Then lead them in the following activity.

IMAGERY:

Close your eyes...and breathe slowly...in...and out... in...and out...and breathe out any tension...tiredness ...distraction you might be feeling at this time(pause) ...On your mental screen create a picture of a machine that could help you do something better...easier... more quickly than before(pause)...What does your machine look like?...Is it made of metal?...wood?...plastic?... aluminum?...steel?...Is there a special company that must build it or can you build it yourself?(pause)...What does your machine do?(pause)...Do you know anyone else who would benefit from your machine?(pause)...Anyone who might not appreciate it?(pause)...Now prepare your-self to come back to this room...On the count of three take a deep breath...hold it...and slowly open your eyes as you exhale...One...two...three...

DISCUSSION:

Describe your machine in detail...shape...size...weight...
   color...use...company (if any) that builds it.
What does it do?
Who benefits by it?
Who doesn't like it? Why?

SUPPLEMENTARY ACTIVITIES:

Art: Have your people draw their machine and label the parts. If this is a drafting class you might have them do this according to certain specifications formulated in drafting theories.

Have people construct their machines from wood, cardboard, paper, etc.

Have them draw their machines on overhead transparencies and show these drawings as "films" to the others.

Writing: Locate companies that could build such machines and have your people send letters suggesting that such machines be built.

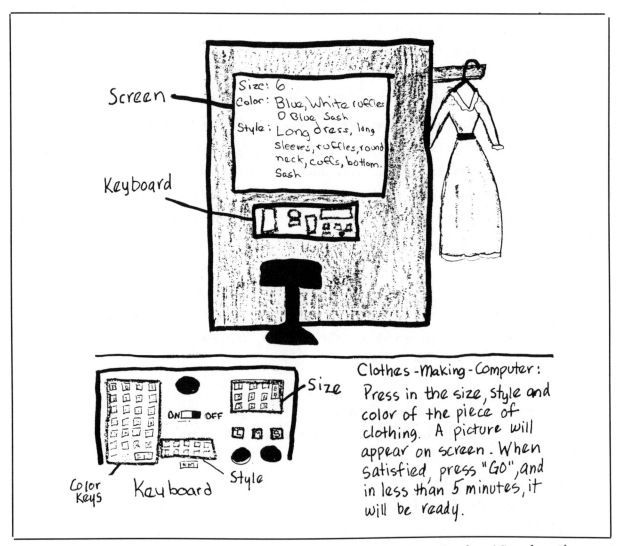

Carla (Grade 8)

DISEASE ... GETTING WELL

PREPARATION:

Discuss concepts related to disease, immunity and getting well. Explain how the body fights disease. Discuss the value of vitamins, good nutrition, rest, and relaxation.

IMAGERY:

Travel inside you body to a place where you can watch your cells interacting with each other (pause)...If your body has an infection and is fighting a disease at this time, you will see healthy and unhealthy cells mingling together..Now picture strong healthy cells filled with powerful light...just like sunlight... fighting off the unhealthy ones...knocking them out...devouring them...destroying them(pause)... This is how your own body fights disease(pause)... Look at your powerful healthy cells and thank them for taking care of you(pause)...Finish this imagery by picturing yourself in perfect health... radiating with beautiful energy(pause)... Now on the count of three...

DISCUSSION:

What do your unhealthy cells look like? Your healthy ones? Describe how your healthy cells conquered the unhealthy ones. Describe yourself radiating with beautiful energy.

SUPPLEMENTARY ACTIVITIES:

Art: Have people draw their healthy cells conquering the unhealthy cells.

Drama: Have people dance and move as if they were healthy cells fighting off the unhealthy ones.

There is a terrible disease attacking the body. A little person who has magic powers zaps the disease with a bright light, killing it.

Carla (Grade 8)

me inside myself with my magic stick and on the end of my magic stick is a colored block that shoots out germ killer and puts magic dust around the disease.

Katy (Grade 8)

FANTASTIC MACHINES

PREPARATION:

Talk about machines that help people live better and improve the quality of life. Ask your people to tell you about their favorite machines and to describe how these machines make their lives happier...easier. Then tell them that they are going to travel away one hundred years into the future and see what new machines have been invented that seem to help people improve the quality of life.

IMAGERY:

Create a time capsule for yourself that will take you one hundred years into the future(pause)... Get into this capsule...blast off...and experience yourself now moving one hundred years into the future ...When your time capsule stops moving you will know you have arrived in the future(pause)...If you haven't yet arrived do so now(pause)...Now leave your capsule and look around...Somewhere you will find a machine... or, perhaps, many machines that seem to help people live happy, healthy and intelligent lives...Look now and find this machine or these machines(pause)...What's happening? ...How are people being helped?(pause)...Prepare yourself now to climb back into your capsule...blast off and return to your home in this year(pause)...Land back here at home and climb out of your capsule(pause)...On the count of three, open your eyes and get ready to draw your machine and to describe what you experienced...One...two...three...

SUPPLEMENTARY ACTIVITY:

Art: Have people draw, paint and/or build their machine.
Draw the machine on an overhead transparency, project it
and have others guess what the machine is and what it can
do.

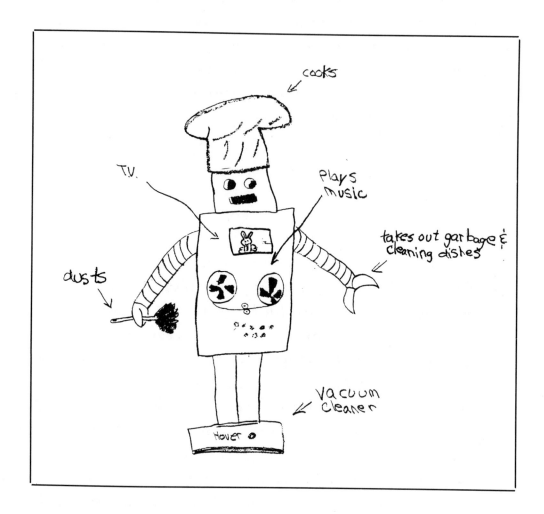

"My machine is every bachelor's dream machine! It cooks gourmet
meals, dusts, vacuums, takes out the garbage, washes the dishes,
and even has a TV and stereo in it, so I can just sit there and
enjoy its company, and feel I'm not alone, but not be stuck with
a naggy wife!"

Michael (Grade 8)

"In the future, we will have machines all over the city streets,
like lampposts. Whenever you're feeling negative or angry or
like you'd really like to bash somebody, all you have to do is
to go and stand in between two of these posts. They will suck
out all the bad vibes, and spray you with a love perfume
that leaves you with positive energies that don't drain you.
These machines will be great, because it's not healthy to keep
stuffing away bad feelings. We just get sick if we do that.
And if we're feeling negative, that's our problem to deal
with, not someone else's to dump it all on. These machines
will make it possible for us to clear out these feelings
without making others suffer."

Michelle (Grade 8)

INNER SPACE OF THE BODY

PREPARATION:

Discuss internal body parts, functions of various organs.
If possible show pictures of these organs, muscles, bones,
circulatory system, and the like.

IMAGERY:

Begin your trip inside of your body...Start at the
top of your head(pause)...descending slowly through
your brain(pause)...moving from side to side to examine
the inside of each ear(pause)...now moving to the
front to examine your eyes(pause)...your nose(pause)...
traveling along your cheeks(pause)...Continue
descending down your neck(pause)...into your chest
(pause)...Notice your lungs(pause)...your heart(pause)...
your ribs(pause)...Now continue descending...
(Direct people to continue this journey as you/they
would like)...On the count of three...

DISCUSSION:

Which body parts fascinate you the most?
Which ones seem more familiar to you? Less familiar?
Do any of them seem to need attention (caring) from you?
If so, which?

VARIATIONS:

Blood Cells: Have people picture themselves as blood cells traveling through the various veins...

Oxygen: Have people picture themselves as oxygen traveling through the blood stream...

Nerve Impulses: Have people picture themselves as nerve impulses responding to stimuli...

Bones: Have people picture themselves as bones...

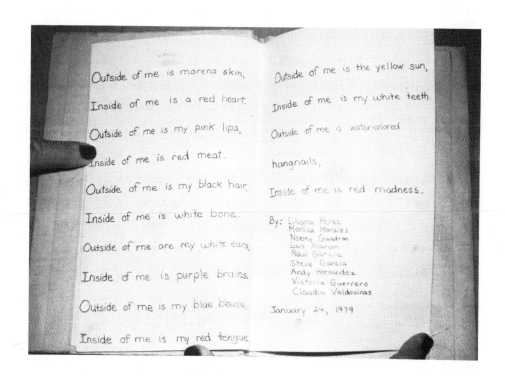

INNER SPACE OF THE BRAIN

PREPARATION:

Discuss parts of the brain such as hemispheres, corpus callosum, lobes, neo-cortex, limbic and neural pathways.

IMAGERY:

Prepare yourself to travel inside your brain (pause)...Slowly, now, enter the top of your head and go into your brain(pause)...Notice the convolutions (pause)...the neural pathways(pause)...Notice the color of your brain(pause)...Now enter the neo-cortex... and travel to the parietal lobe(pause)...then to the occipital(pause)...then to the temporal(pause)... and upward to the frontal lobes(pause)...What **do you see...feel...smell...taste...experience in each one?**(pause)...Now find the corpus callosum and slide across from one hemisphere to the other... What does this feel like?(pause)...Now enter your right hemisphere...What do you experience there? (pause)...Now enter your left hemisphere(pause)... What do you experience there?(pause)...Now compare your experiences in each hemisphere...Are there similarities?...Differences?(pause)...Now travel to the limbic area of each hemisphere where emotion centers are located...What do you experience in your emotional centers?(pause)...Now take one last look at you entire brain and thank it for serving you so well(pause)...On the count of three...

DISCUSSION:

Have your people discuss the questions posed in the imagery activity.

172

INNER SPACE OF THE MIND

PREPARATION:

Ask people to give their opinions as to what mind is...where it exists...when and how it manifests...how it influences behavior...if there is such a thing as a "good mind" and/or a "bad mind".

SUGGESTED MUSIC:

2001: Space Odyssey; Snowflakes Are Dancing by Tomita.

IMAGERY:

Travel now deep within yourself...and find
a place of wonderful peace and quiet...
where everything is calm...wonderful...pleasant
(pause)...Allow these feelings of calmness to flow
throughout your body until you feel deeply relaxed
(pause)...Ask an inner guide to help you, to lead
you to where you can experience your mind(pause)..
And with the assistance and wisdom of this guide go
now and visit your mind(pause)...Where are you?
(pause)...What does your mind look like?...Feel like?
...Are there any sounds?(pause)...Are there things you
don't recognize?...don't understand?(pause)...If so ask
your guide to assist you to better understand
what you are experiencing(pause)...Prepare yourself
to complete this experience and return to us
here in the room...fully refreshed...and ready to
work with this imagery(pause)...On the count of three...

SUPPLEMENTARY ACTIVITIES:

Poetry: Have people write a poem (i.e., Haiku, Cinquain) describing their experience.

Art: Have people draw their minds..what they saw... experienced...heard...felt.

VARIATION:

The MANDALA is a series of concentric forms. It is a universal symbol inherent in man's consciousness, and has existed in constructions, rituals, and art forms throughout many civilizations. It is often used to represent the mind, for it is a universal symbol of harmony and perfect balance.

To draw a mandala, we start by centering ourselves and then slowly begin to journey within ourselves until we reach the mind. When we arrive at the mind, we are in the center of it, focusing out onto all regions of our mind. Soon we see colors, textures, images, symbols, lines, various shapes going from us at center to all areas of the mind. Later we draw what we have seen and experienced within us. This drawing, our very own Mandala, is a wonderful symbol of who we are.

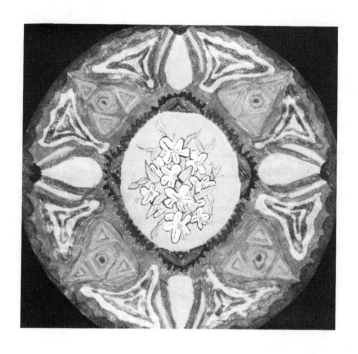

"My mandala has white lilies in the center and colored shields on the outside protecting the lilies. The lilies are delicate and sensitive, and are used around Easter time. They represent new life. But new life is always in need of protection and care. The purple shields represent the security I feel from my parents and teachers who care about me and help me grow. The green and blue shields are my good friends who help me feel important. The yellow represents fun. I like to have good times. I like my life just how it is right now. I know I will grow and change just like all beautiful flowers."

Joyce (Grade 8)

175

IN THE WOMB

PREPARATION:

Discuss with your people the current research that suggests that we can actually remember things that happened while in our mother's womb.

NOTE: If this imagery is presented in a sex education or science class, you might want to include a presentation of body organs and their functions.

IMAGERY:

Close your eyes...breathe in...and out...in...and out...relax your body(pause)...Now imagine moving back in time until you are very little...in fact so little that you are a developing fetus in your mother's womb(pause)...Feel the warmth of her womb surrounding you...and feel the sensations of safety...security...and gentle rocking(pause)... As a fetus...notice whether you can hear your mother's heartbeat or any sounds outside of your dark environment...Notice any conversation you may hear...or sensations of your mother that you may feel(pause)...Now prepare yourself to leave the womb...and return to us here in the room(pause)... Be aware of the sounds and feelings of this room (pause)...On the count of three take a deep breath ...exhale...and open your eyes ready to write and talk about your experience...One...two...three...

DISCUSSION:

Describe the womb in detail.
What were you doing in the womb?
Could you feel the rhythm of your mother's movements?
Could you hear her heartbeat?
Describe any conversations you heard going on outside the womb.

OUTER SPACE TRAVEL

PREPARATION:

Discuss ideas related to outer space such as planets, asteroids, comets. Discuss outer space travel. Play musical themes appropriate to outer space and discuss what types of images come to mind while they are listening to the music.

SUGGESTED MUSIC:

2001: Space Odyssey, Planets by Tomita, Starborn Suite by Steve Halpern.

IMAGERY:

Imagine yourself traveling through space. You are well protected and don't have to worry about oxygen, food, falling asteroids, space rocks...You won't have any trouble finding your way back to earth... Now gently lift off the earth and with the speed of light travel through space(pause)...Go farther and farther and deeper and deeper into space... What do you see?...Hear?...Smell?(pause)...What does the atmosphere feel like?(pause)...Stop along the way and visit the stars and suns...Remember that you are fully protected so you don't have to worry about being burned(pause)...Now visit some planets...What do you experience there?(pause)...Finish your visit, now, and turn back toward earth(pause)...What does the earth look like from outer space?(pause)...As you get closer and closer to earth how does it look?(pause)...Now pick a spot to land and slow yourself down...slower... ...slower...slower...now gently land(pause)...On the count of three...

SUPPLEMENTARY ACTIVITIES:

Art: Have people draw or paint their experiences.

Poetry: Have people write poems (i.e., Haiku, Cinquain) describing their experiences.

Peace

I went out to look for peace and then I found hate, and in my own planet, I found some kind of magical future. I found freedom, and I didn't find hate or sorrow. I was happy here. I wanted to stay, because in the other world there was war, and hate and sorrow, and I didn't like it there. I can go to my magical planet and find peace and freedom.

Kim (Grade 6)

"Above the stars lies a mystery moon.
Above the moon is a wind of silence.
Above the wind is a field of flowers.
Above the flowers lies eternity and imagination for the future.

Cindy (Grade 6)

"Above the sky, across the sea,
There I walked for eternity - to see
What makes the sky blue, what makes the sea flow.
Seeking one solution for everything.
What could it be?

Tina (Grade 6)

179

"Above the sky the endless stars shine.
Above the rain the sky darkens.
Above the universe the earth turns.
Under the rainbow a unicorn flew past my imagination.

Above the sky to a land of love
Above the universe where the land of endless things never ends.
Above myself lives the endless sky
I want to reach.

Oanh Pham (Grade 6)

POSSIBLE HUMAN

PREPARATION:

Have your people talk about projections concerning human capabilities in the future. How will intelligence change? What will the presence of computers free us to do? To become? What new physical mind skills will people develop as our brains continue to develop?

IMAGERY:

Close your eyes and travel away into the future...
to a future where humans have developed new capacities
...new physical abilities..new intellectual abilities
...Watch what people are doing at this time(pause)...
What do people look like?(pause)...Are there any
talents people have at this time that were only
speculative or imagined as possible realities back in
_____(indicate whatever year you are presently in)?
(pause)...What are you able to do at this time that
you weren't able to do back in _____?(pause)...Do
people seem to be using these new capabilities for
helpful purposes?...Are there any problems posed by
these capabilities?(pause)...Is life better because
of these new capabilities?(pause)...Prepare yourself
to come back to us here in the room and work with your
experiences...On the count of three...

QUESTIONS:

Describe your "possible human".
What new physical...intellectual capabilities does he/she have?
Does life seem to be better at this time?

In this activity, students work in pairs. One person sits quietly while the other person looks deeply into their partner's mind and tries to read the person's images of the future. They then trace the profile of the person and write their thoughts on the drawing. This particular drawing was done by a sixth grade girl...

Amy Lee - what her world will be like!

Amy's world is opening up, especially in the last year, to many new experiences that are expanding her consciousness. I sense that she will not only continue in this direction, but she has indicated that she wants to help others in these directions as well. To me she is already a person of planetary awareness approaching the universal. Her life, I believe, will be increasingly devoted to the well being of all humanity.

"The Possible Human" through the eyes of Angela (adult) ...

PROTECTOR CELLS

PREPARATION:

Discuss the role of white blood cells in helping to fight disease.

IMAGERY:

Go inside your body to a place where you can watch your cells(pause)...Find all the white blood cells...the ones that protect you from disease...and picture them as warriors..ready to fight off any germs that try to enter the body (pause)...Picture your special protector cells with much light around them and notice how they use this light to fight off any germs(pause)... Travel through your entire body, now, and find these special protector cells wherever you go (pause)...Anytime you are afraid you might get sick...or you might pick up germs that could hurt you...call upon these protector cells to help you(pause)...On the count of three...

DISCUSSION:

Describe your protector (white) cells.
How do they fight off disease (germs)?

SUPPLEMENTARY ACTIVITY:

Art: Have people draw these protector cells keeping away germs. If there is ever an epidemic of colds, flu, measles and the like you might have people draw these protector cells and hang them around the room as a symbol of protection. For younger children, you might have them wear these protector cells around their neck or pinned to them.

Emily (Grade 8)

STARS

PREPARATION:

Discuss the properties of stars, what they are composed of, how they behave. Ask people to share their experiences of stargazing.

SUGGESTED MUSIC:

Spectrum Suite and Starborn Suite by Steve Halpern.

IMAGERY:

Climb into a specially designed space ship and travel away to the heavens where you see hundreds of stars (pause)...Notice what everything looks like as you get closer to the stars(pause)...Find one star that looks interesting to you and land on it...You are protected by a special space suit so you don't need to worry about getting burned...or poisoned by gases(pause)...Look around...What do you see?(pause)...Does anything look familiar to you?(pause)...What colors do you see?(pause) ...Do you smell...taste anything?(pause)...What are you feeling as you look around this star?(pause)...Now listen carefully and see if you hear anything?(pause)... or is everything quiet?(pause)...Prepare yourself now to return to earth(pause)...Climb back into your space-ship...blast off...and return to us here on earth(pause) ...five...four...three...two...one...zero...Now you've landed(pause)...Open your eyes...fully refreshed... feeling great...and ready to work with your experiences.

SUPPLEMENTARY ACTIVITIES:

> Art: Have people draw and/or paint their trip.

> Have people draw and/or paint their star, highlighting what it looks like on the inside.

> Make stars from paper mache, construction paper, cardboard, etc. and color them as they were experienced. Then hang them around the room as mobiles.

VARIATION:

> Have people "take photographs of what they saw on the star" and bring these photos back to earth. They then use colors to draw these photos and display them around the room.

Grade 2 students

A CINQUAIN ...

Sun

Hot, bright

Burning, shining, flaring

Lights up my day

Star

(Allyson, Grade 10)

186

STRETCHING OUR CAPABILITIES
(Using Our Kinesthetic Body)

PREPARATION:

You'll need to decide some criterion for this exercise, something the person wasn't able to do before the exercise, but will be able to do after it, such as touching their toes, the floor, a mark on a wall, a string hung across the room. Your people will need to test their abilities prior to the imagery.

(For this imagery we will work with "touching toes/floor") Bend down and see how far you can touch. Note if you can touch your knees, shins, ankles, floor, flatten your hands on the floor. Note how far you go and be sure that you do this without straining yourself. As soon as you feel pain or discomfort stop and note how far you've gone.

IMAGERY:

Close your eyes and relax your entire body...Take a slow deep breath...and exhale any tiredness or tension you may be feeling(pause)...Feel yourself light...floating ...deeply relaxed(pause)...(Repeat the relaxation procedure two more times or as needed)...Now picture yourself on a warm sunny day...feeling the sun's rays penetrating and warming your entire body...especially your back...legs and feet(pause)...Your body seems very loose...just like rubber...and you feel very relaxed... centered(pause)...Now picture yourself laying in the sun...on your stomach...soaking up the warm rays on your back and legs...loosening up your muscles(pause) ...A friend offers to massage your back and legs, and as this person massages you...you have the feeling that your legs and back are stretching...getting longer(pause) ...Your friend finishes this massage and you feel very

187

light...almost airy...so you decide to get up and run...
As you are running you notice how loose your muscles
feel...especially the muscles in your back and legs
(pause)...Your whole body is very relaxed(pause)...
Stop running now...rest a little...and touch your toes
(or floor)...You can go as far as you want because
every muscle is like rubber...See yourself doing this
now(pause)...Do it again...and again...See how great it
feels to be so loose...tension free(pause)...Now open
your eyes and touch your toes (floor, etc.) here in this
room. (Watch and see how many people go farther. Most
people have great success with this exercise.)
Now let's talk about what happened...

NOTE: If some people didn't go farther suggest they
practice the imagery on their own and try the experience
again.

DISCUSSION:

Show us how far you went the first time...then show us
how far you went after the imagery.

If you can do so well touching your toes, what other things
might you do better by creating an image of success in your
mind (i.e., taking tests, hitting a baseball, giving oral
reports, keeping calm in moments of conflict, etc.)?

VARIATION:

If you have some people who have mastered a skill and others
who haven't, ask those who have to visualize the others
successfully performing the skill. For example, suppose some
of your people have learned a new piece of music very quickly.
You have them image the others learning it quickly.

189

TIME

PREPARATION:

Conduct a discussion on time, what it is and what it does. Ask your people to describe how they experience time. What do past time...future time mean? How would they measure time if they were not able to use clocks or any of the conventional methods familiar to us today?

IMAGERY:

In this imagery activity, we will travel to the world of time...our personal world of time. Close your eyes and take a slow...deep breath (continue relaxation procedures)...Now find a special machine or suit that will help you travel with ease to your world of time (pause)...Slowly take off from the earth and begin your journey into time...Notice everything you see along the way...Is it dark?...light?...warm?...cold?...Are you in outer space?...in water?...Are there stars?...planets? different forms of life or other worlds?(pause)...Ahead of you is your land of time, so go there now...When you arrive there, explore the land with each of your senses... Notice what you can see...hear...touch or feel...smell... taste...What shapes are there?...Are there people?... buildings?...machines?...What kinds of activities are going on?...(You have one minute of clock time which is all the time you need to explore your world of time.) ...Before you return to earth, let your body feel the rhythm of time in your land...Is time fast?...slow?... marching?...running?...flowing?...dancing?...standing still?...leaping?...How is time moving?(pause)...It's time to return to us here in the room (space, place, etc.)...so take one last look at your world of time... feel your rhythm of time in your body...and return here to us (pause)...On the count of three...

190

DISCUSSION:

Have your people discuss the questions posed in the imagery activity.

SUPPLEMENTARY ACTIVITY:

Art: Have people draw their perceptions of time.

Movement: Have people dance-move to their perceptions of time. Those who see time as linear may make marching type movements, whereas those who perceive time as flowing or circular motion may make wave-like movements.

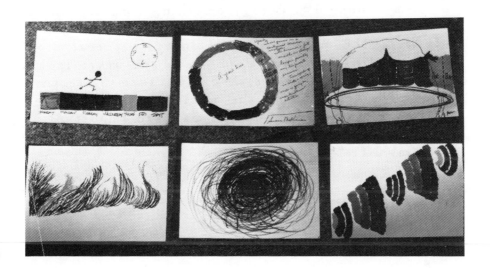

Comments of Adult Education Students (Top row, left to right):

"It seems as though I am always on a schedule with one eye watching the clock, and the other looking at the calendar, running to meet classes, appointments, etc.

"Time passes in a continual circular motion. The summer and fall months are always longer - possibly my two favorite seasons. Time speeds up in winter and spring. More is going on and there are more deadlines and activities."

"There is a definite image of the days of the week that I have had for as long as I remember. It is an eliptical movement into my periferal vision on each side, with weekends being at both ends. Wednesday sticks up in the middle and Tuesday and Thursday are connectors. Monday is blue and down and Friday is bright and up."

(Bottom row, left to right):

"Pattern of time, repetitive in degree, new happenings or thoughts coming in, then the repetition of pattern, then change again."

"Time began structured, but as life continues, time is ever expanding and free flowing, with intermittent periods of intensity or structure/confinement."

"The colors represent how I feel about how I'm spending my time. When I'm doing something I really enjoy, my energy field sparkles with bright color, and time just seems to fly. When what I'm doing is a real drag to me, I get feeling low, and depressed, and start looking on the dark side of things, and time seems interminable. Looking at my life on the whole, however, I feel like both the good times and the bad are important, because I learn from everything I do, and everything that comes into my life."

NOTE:

We have heard from many teachers and counselors that people who tend to experience time as a non-linear, more "here and now" spontaneous flow of energy (such as we see in the bottom row of drawings), often feel that schools discriminate against them by not respecting their inner rhythm, demanding instead that they adhere to rigid time blocks for classes, and timed objective-type tests.

TIME MACHINE: FUTURE TIME

PREPARATION:

It is suggested you precede this imagery with the one on "Time" so as to give your people the opportunity to better understand how they each experience time. Discuss the word "future" and ask people to tell you what images they associate with future. Have them think back to people who lived two or three centuries ago and discuss whether people at that time imagined the realities we have today such as fuel powered cars...jet engines...computers...kidney/heart/lung machines and the like. In what way do we carry within us blueprints for the future? Can we know the future by becoming more aware of our own inner images, sensations and feelings?

SUGGESTED MUSIC:

2001: Space Odyssey or Starborn Suite by Halpern.

IMAGERY:

Create a time machine that will take you 1,000 years
into the future(pause)...Climb into this machine and
let it take you 1000 years into the future...Note any
bodily sensations you have...emotional reactions...images
...All of these are an important part of your experience
with future time and you have nothing to fear(pause)...
Slowly make your time machine come to a full stop and
prepare yourself to climb out into future time(pause)...
Leave the machine and begin looking around
Note everything you see...hear...touch...feel...smell...
taste(pause)...What are people doing, if there are
people?(pause)...What form of transportation is available,
if there is transportation?(pause)...Are there schools?...
grocery stores?...department stores?...shopping centers?...

193

police stations?...fire stations?...churches?...apartment buildings?...condos?...public parks?(pause)...Now pay attention to how people relate to each other...What do you notice?(pause)...Now turn your attention inward...to your own thoughts and feelings about what is going on(pause)... What is happening in you as you experience future time? (pause)...Now prepare yourself to return to present time (pause)...Climb back into your time machine...leave future time...and gently land here in the present(pause)... When you are ready, take a slow deep breath...open your eyes...and be fully refreshed and ready to work with your experiences.

DISCUSSION:

Have your people answer the questions indicated in the imagery. Is there anything in the world now that looks like the things you saw in the future?

Are there any movies, books, or novels that depict the future, such as you just experienced it?

SUPPLEMENTARY ACTIVITIES:

Art: Have people make a mural of their trip to future time. Have them construct a time machine from wood, cardboard, etc.

Writing: Have them write brief accounts of their experiences and illustrate (draw/paint) these experiences on the same sheet.

VARIATION 1:

Change time to 100, 500, 2,000 years into the future.

VARIATION 2:

Change imagery to past time. Travel 1,000 years (100, 500, 2,000) back into the past.

UNDERWATER VOYAGE

PREPARATION:

Ask your people if any of them skin or scuba dive, or if they have seen pictures of underwater life. You might make available pictures or other visuals of underwater life in an ocean, lake or river.

IMAGERY:

Today we are going on an underwater voyage. Decide whether you want to go to the ocean, the lake or a river(pause)...Close your eyes and take a slow, deep breath, hold it...and exhale any tiredness, distraction you might be feeling at this time(pause)...(Repeat as needed.)...Now create a diving suit for yourself.. something that will protect you under the water...You might also want to give yourself fins, a face mask, a snorkel and/or oxygen tank...or if you are going very deep...you might need a special diving machine to take you down(pause)...Begin your descent into the water and look around at the underwater life...What do you see? ...hear?...feel?...taste?...smell?(pause)...Notice the the fish...plants...rocks...colors...anything else you see...You have one minute of clock time which is all the time you need to explore underwater life(pause)...Now prepare yourself to return to us here in the room, fully alert...refreshed and ready to work with this imagery... On the count of three...

DISCUSSION:

Describe your diving gear. What did you wear?

What was it like descending through the water?

What did you see? hear? touch? feel? smell? taste?

Did anything exciting or unusual happen while you were under water?

SUPPLEMENTARY ACTIVITIES

Art: Have your people draw or make murals of their underwater voyage. They can also create objects that they saw and place these in a large aquarium or tank created by the whole class. Have them make these objects and hang them around the room as mobiles.

Writing: Have them write creative compositions about their voyage.

Poetry: Have them write short poems describing their adventures.

VARIATION:

Use this activity in conjunction with the study of marine life, marine biology, famous underwater scientists such as Jacques Cousteau, historical or storybook characters such as Black Beard the Pirate, for underwater treasure hunts and the like.

These composition/posters were done by French II students in conjunction with their study of Jacques Cousteau ...

"I wrapped myself in a silver cloud. It was cold and wet. I felt safe and sure of myself inside the cloud. I saw multi-colored fish - sharks, seals, sea lions, dolphins, an octopus and a whale. I discovered a beautiful cavern decorated with different colored flowers from the sea. The inside of the cavern was filled with jewels. Fantasy and imagination were the most important aspects of my trip. It was a very beautiful experience. When I played with the dangerous sharks and whales, I was fascinated."

Diane (Grade 11)

"I felt very relaxed and fresh. I swam and danced to
music, and I met with the sea horses, some fish and
dolphins. Then I became a part of all this. I became
a real mermaid. The dolphins took me to King Neptune's
castle where he offered me a chest full of goldand
jewels if I would stay there with him. I explained
to him that it wasn't possible, because I would be
away from my family and friends. We never spoke a word
during this conversation. We communicated telepathi-
cally. The castle was made from pearls and was sort
of an albacore color.

Then I departed from the depths of the sea.
While leaving the sea, I lost my form of a mermaid,
and I felt the feeling of the air on my body and the
warmth of the sun, too! I continued my journey back
to my own home while waving goodbye to the mysteries
of the ocean."

Lorene (Grade 11)

CHAPTER EIGHT

GUIDED AFFECTIVE IMAGERIES

These imageries help develop the deeply personal skills of introspection, self-reflection, self-understanding, bonding, unity, trust, love, conflict resolution, synergic problem solving, empathy, community, communication and self-determined self-concept. They serve to nurture emotional maturity by targeting the symbiotic relationship between emotions, thoughts, attitudes, behaviors and physical-mental well being.

The imageries in this section are arranged thematically, and are not necessarily meant to be used in the order in which they appear.

BEFORE YOU BEGIN, PLEASE REMEMBER TO ...

☐ Prepare your people by discussing the importance of using the particular imagery at this time.

☐ Check to see if they need any movement types of activities to help settle and center their energy.

☐ Check to see if they need a focusing activity to sharpen their inner vision.

☐ Make alternate work available in case you have individuals who do not want to do the imagery activity.

☐ Prepare any needed materials such as crayons, paints, paper ahead of time.

☐ Read the imagery in its entirety and change the wording and pauses to meet the maturity, readiness, interest and proficiency levels of your group.

☐ Include a deep breathing/centering exercise to begin the imagery.

☐ If the imagery does not include a form for ending the activity (i.e., the "countdown and return to the room"), be sure you have one ready. You can look at the chapter on Getting Started for ideas.

☐ Consider adding multi-sensory suggestions such as "What do you see?...hear?...feel?...smell?...taste? ..." whenever you wish to heighten the sensory experience even if they are not included in the actual text of the imagery.

APPRECIATIONS

PREPARATION:

Discuss the idea of "appreciations" with your people and ask them to talk about times when they've felt deeply appreciated by others, and when they've appreciated others.

IMAGERY:

Close your eyes and take a slow, deep breath...Hold it...
Now exhale with a slight sigh and breathe out any tiredness, tension or distractions you might be feeling at
this time (pause)...Do this again. Take a slow, deep
breath...Hold it...Now exhale with a slight sigh and
breathe out any tiredness, tension or distractions you
might be feeling(pause)...Now travel away to a place that
you find very beautiful and experience it with all of
your senses...Note the things you see (pause)...smell...
(pause)...hear (pause)...feel (pause)...taste (pause)...
touch (pause)...In a few moments you will see some people
who deeply appreciate you...who recognize how great you
are and who wish to thank you for being you...Look around
at this time. See these people coming to show you their
appreciation (pause)...Listen to what they tell you (pause)
...If no one comes to you at this time just know that you
are the source of your own appreciation for now, and you
do not need others to come to you...Now talk with each
person who comes to you...thank them for their appreciation...and ask them if they can tell you any special
things about yourself (pause)...Complete these conversations and prepare yourself to come back to us here in the
room...fully alert...refreshed...and ready to work with
the imagery (pause)...On the count of three take a slow,
deep breath...Hold it...And open your eyes while exhaling.
One...two...

DISCUSSION:

Who came to appreciate you? Does this person (Do these persons) ordinarily appreciate you in real life?

To whom did you show appreciation? Do you usually show appreciation to this person (these persons)?

What was said to you by this person (these persons)?

What did you say?

SUPPLEMENTARY ACTIVITIES:

Art: Have your people draw and/or paint the person(s) who came to them and write on the drawing what the person(s) said.

Writing:

Have each person write out their appreciation on a large piece of paper and post these around the room.

Have each person print their appreciation on an index card and wear it for the day.

Have each person write a first person letter to themselves beginning with "I appreciate you because..."!

Have each person write letters to others in the class (or to those whom they saw in their imagery) beginning with "I appreciate you because..."!

Have your people write messages of appreciation to each other in the group, and fix these on the backs of each person. Individuals try to guess what messages have been written to them on their back. Once they guess correctly, they can remove the messages.

Drama: Have your people work as partners or in groups of three to four. One person receives compliments from the others. Continue doing this until each person has had a chance to receive compliments from the others.

"I like you because you are my mother and you are happy.
I like you because you are my father and you are just and
sensitive. I like you because you are my sister, and you
are generous and happy. I like you because you are my grandmother and you are wise and calm."

Susan (Grade 9 - French I)

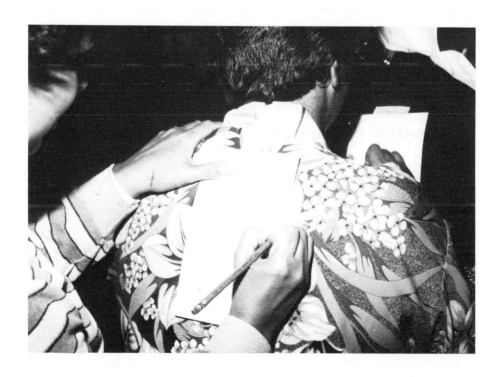

CHANGING UNWANTED FEELINGS

PREPARATION:

Discuss the importance of owning feelings and making them okay to have. What's most important is that we allow ourselves to feel whatever it is we are experiencing. We aren't stuck with negative feelings, however, and can use the power of positive energy-positive imaging to change any negative feelings to positive ones.

IMAGERY:

Allow yourself to fully experience a feeling that you don't like...one that annoys you(pause)... Now take this feeling and go away to a place where everyone is feeling the same way(pause)... Be sure that you are in this scene with the others...experiencing it fully (pause)...Now back away or out of this scene and move to a place where you can observe the scene from a distance. Notice what the situation looks like when you remove yourself from it(pause)...Now think of an opposite feeling...a positive one that counteracts... transforms...or removes the unwanted feeling... What positive feeling are you concentrating on? (pause)...Now take this feeling and visualize it spreading throughout this place...covering everyone and everything...transforming the entire scene with its powerfully positive energy(pause)... It's time for you to enter the scene...so do this now...Become a part of the environment and let yourself experience the full impact of this wonderful positive energy that has completely filled your place (pause)...Let this feeling permeate your being...

feel it everywhere in your body...in your mind...
throughout your emotions...uplifting your spirit
(pause)...Enjoy this feeling of well being initiated by
this positive emotion(pause)...If there is anyone you
know whom you think would benefit from being in this
wonderfully nurturing situation, bring them in at this
time and watch them experience the beautiful energy
generated by your powerfully positive emotion(pause)...
Remember to do this anytime you feel the need to lift
yourself out of negativity or unwanted, depressing
feelings(pause)...Prepare yourself now to return to
us here in the room...fully refreshed...renewed...
ready to work with the imagery experience (pause)...
On the count of three...

DISCUSSION:

What negative or unpleasant emotion did you choose to work
with?

Describe how you felt while carrying this emotion within you.

What did the scene...others...look like while being flooded
with this unwanted feeling?

What positive emotion did you select to counteract the negative
emotion?

Describe what happened to the scene...others...when you filled
the place with your powerfully positive emotion.

SUPPLEMENTARY ACTIVITY:

Art: Have people draw the situation as they experienced it
with the unwanted emotion. Then have them draw it as they
experienced it with the positive emotion.

CHOOSING A TOTEM

PREPARATION:

Discuss the meaning of "totems" in ancient cultures. Stress the idea that totems, usually animal symbols, were considered to be the lifelong protector of people, and the personality traits of the totem reflected important personality traits of the recipient. Very often it was the totem itself that guided, directed, protected and inspired the individual throughout life. Totems were given to individuals by a wise person such as a Medicine Man or Woman revered as a mediator between the gods and people by members of a tribe or clan.

IMAGERY:

Picture yourself as seven years old(pause). Somewhere around you, you will find a person who looks very wise...and who seems to know you quite well... Greet this person and ask him or her to tell you his or her name(pause)...Ask them to give you your own special totem...the animal symbol that will give you strength...and will help you to always make good decisions about your life ...What animal totem is given to you?(pause)...Do you recognize this animal? (pause)...Ask this Wise Person to describe the animal totem to you by telling you how you and the animal are alike. For example, if your Wise Person gave you a lion, the Person might say "The lion is smart and very strong, and you are smart and very strong...The lion protects its young and you protect younger children whom you love and care for."(pause)...Now ask your totem if there is anything you need to know right now to be happy...secure...and to sense that your life is deeply meaningful to you (pause)...On the count of three take a deep breath...hold it...and exhale with a slight sigh...

DISCUSSION:

Describe the person who came to you. Do you recognize the person?

What animal **totem** did the person give you?

How are you like your **totem**?

"My **totem** is a German Shepherd Dog. The dog is beautiful and seems to like everyone. He ran around the yard barking gently at our neighbors and started licking everyone's hands. People think he is very gentle and loves them all. My Wise Person told me that the shepherd and I were very much alike. Here's what he said:

'Your German Shepherd is friendly and cares for everyone. He protects the neighbors as well as your family. He is smart and very observant of what's going on. He knows how to protect people without a whole lot of fighting. In fact, he is quite a peaceful dog and prefers to love people rather than biting them. Denise, you really care for the welfare of other people, too, and you are very protective of them. But you are gentle, and have the gift of helping others feel loved and cared for and safe. Use your intelligence to accomplish things without getting into fights and ripping people apart'."

SUPPLEMENTARY ACTIVITIES:

Art: Have people draw and or paint their **totems**. They might want to wear them around their necks.

Make the totems out of cardboard, wood, soap and display in the room. Build a totem pole from the individual totems.

Movement: People become their totems and dance as those totems.

VARIATION:

Suggest that the **totems** be any symbol such as flowers, vegetables or aspects of the sky and planets.

I go through life ...

- as a rabbit, gentle and white (Adriana)
- as a bird that always flies around peacefully (Cindy)
- as a bull, rough and tough (Michelle)

My Spirit

There is a fox in me, a sneaky silver fox
I wander around the forest as sly as I can be.
I look for shelter when I'm frightened.
I like sneaking around looking for fun.
I'm glad to be wild and free.

There's also a tiger in me, a beautiful
   striped tiger.
I'm big and scary. I prowl the jungle.
I love climbing trees.
I'm glad I'm free.

Kim (Grade 6)

" My totem is an eagle. Initially, I formed a chicken, but my
logical mind rejected that symbol as fear. So I changed it
to a dove which symbolizes love to me. Finally, I changed it
to the eagle which is my true symbol, but which incorporates
fear and love. The eagle's sight is so intense that it flies
high in order not to intimidate others with its piercing eyes.
Thus it creates an impression of aloneness - my fear. However,
I have flown with my eagle in the past. I have burrowed into
the white breast feathers and felt the warmth, comfort, security
and love. Flying with the eagle gives me the opportunity to
explore higher consciousness.

In my meditation, I asked the eagle if I would be alone. I
was filled with an incredible loving feeling around my heart,
and I was shown another eagle with whom I could soar, with
whom I can create, and with whom I can contribute to the world."

Cathy (adult)

" My kitty appeared as a sign to me of the strengths I need in
my life. The kitty represents sensuousness and relaxation.
He has a pink mouth, representing spirituality. His mouth
is wide open, yawning and stretching, completely relaxed.
He is at peace. He sleeps peacefully much of the day, goes
with whoever and whatever comes along in his life and succeeds
at being strong, clean, healthy, without laboring.

   He is alone and is at peace and happy with being alone. He
is with whoever comes along completely. He can snuggle down,
play with, completely enjoy. He doesn't strive - he has it all!

   I'm striving and can't get there - and know he's doing it
right - I needed him!! "

Liz (adult)

COLOR OF LOVE

PREPARATION:

Ask your people to talk about love...feelings of love such as was indicated for the imagery "Love". Then ask them what colors they ordinarily associate with love, if any. Are there certain colors that society usually ascribes to love or feelings of love? Do these colors differ from culture to culture?

IMAGERY:

Imagine yourself here in this room. You notice that the room feels like it is filled with love...Everyone seems to be in a loving mood...Look around the room and see how everyone looks while feeling this loving mood(pause) ...How are people talking with one another while being in a loving mood?(pause)...Suddenly you look around the room and these feelings of love are changing to a color or perhaps to many colors...What colors do you see? ... Now see the entire room filled with these colors, the walls, ceiling, floor, desks, bulletin boards, all of us here in the room(pause)...Look at certain people and notice if they seem to have a specific color around them. Do some people seem to show a specific color for love?(pause)...If there is anyone in your life whom you would like to be here sharing these colors of love and loving feelings, picture them here with us at this time(pause) ...Prepare yourself now to return to us here in the room...fully alert and refreshed, ready to work with this imagery...On the count of three...

DISCUSSION:

What colors did you feel coming from you?

What colors did you notice in the room?

Did certain people in the room seem to have specific colors coming from them?

NOTE:

It's interesting to have people compare what colors they saw around themselves and others. Sometimes we find a high correlation among various people's perceptions of certain colors. Sometimes we also find that certain colors predominate in specific areas of the room. For example, many people seated in one corner of the room will see or feel greens whereas people in another corner might see or feel reds.

VARIATION #1:

You may wish to have your people experience colors for other feelings such as "joy", "trust", "wisdom", "security", "appreciation" and the like. Replace "love" with any of these words.

VARIATION #2:

It's an interesting experience to have people also experience the various senses, such as the "sounds of love". Repeat the imagery "Color of Love" and replace the word "color" with the word "sounds", "taste", "feel", etc.

SUPPLEMENTARY ACTIVITIES:

Art: Give your people colors, watercolors, chalks or other art supplies and have them make murals of what the room looked like filled with the color of love.

Poetry: Have them write poems about the "color of love".

"Love is as fragile as an ant -
    one slight error and it would
    be finished.
Love is as precious as silk,
    but one rip and it is ruined.
Love is as solid as cement.
    Once two people are joined by love
    No other living creature can interfere."
                    Ronnie (Grade 6)

"Love is a fragrance that will never die.
    You can capture this fragrance if you're
    in love, but remember, only if you're
    in love.
If you pretend that you're in love, you
    may smell this beautiful fragrance,
    but you cannot capture it."
                    Michelle (Grade 6)

FEELING FEELINGS

PREPARATION:

Have people discuss various emotions that they experience
in their lives such as joy, anger, security, sadness,
loneliness, togetherness, anxiety, "uptight", appreciation.
Have them write down one emotion they would like to work
with in the imagery.

IMAGERY:

Travel now to a land where everyone and everything
is behaving like your emotion...If you've chosen
joy then everyone and everything will be acting
joyfully...If you've chosen anxiety then everyone
and everything will look anxious...uptight(pause)...
Look carefully at the place...Is there a color that
dominates?(pause)...What do the people look like?...
How are they behaving?...What are they talking
about?(pause)...What do buildings...clothes...cars
...look like?(pause)...Now walk among the people...
What do you feel like when you are with them?(pause)
...Does this place remind you of any places or
situations in your real life?(pause)...Do you
ever act like those people?...If so when?(pause)...
Do you like being in this place?(pause)...Prepare
yourself now to return to us here in the room...
fully refreshed and ready to discuss this experience
(pause)...On the count of three...

DISCUSSION:

Describe your place in detail; i.e., feelings, colors, people,
buildings, atmosphere, etc.

If you liked being in this place what can you do to be there more often?

If you didn't like being there, what can you do to avoid going there again?

Feelings

Feelings are a strong something inside of you. Feelings can make you feel sad or mad, happy or cheerful. Sometimes I like feelings but sometimes I don't. Sometimes I think that people are just one big feeling.

Bobbie (Grade 6)

FEELING GREAT

PREPARATION:

Ask your people to describe how they feel when they are "feeling great." Have them complete sentences such as "My body feels ____." "My mind feels ____." "I'm usually doing ____."

IMAGERY:

Picture yourself feeling wonderful...Health is pulsing through your body...You feel good all over...strong... healthy...relaxed...centered...You have one minute of clock time which is all the time you need to experience yourself feeling great(pause)...Now take a look at the food you eat...What foods help you to feel great?(pause)...Now look at what you are doing... What activities help you to feel great?(pause)... Is there anything else you are doing that helps you feel great? Perhaps you are relaxing at the beach... listening to special music...visiting with a good friend...off by yourself in the woods(pause)...On the count of three take a deep breath...

DISCUSSION:

Have your people describe their experience. Whatever they experienced is okay!

How was your body feeling? Your mind?

What foods make you feel great? Activities? Other?

SUPPLEMENTARY ACTIVITIES:

   Art: Have your people draw themselves feeling great. Cut
      out their drawings and place them around the room.
   Drama: Have your people dance out their feelings about
      their own wellbeing.

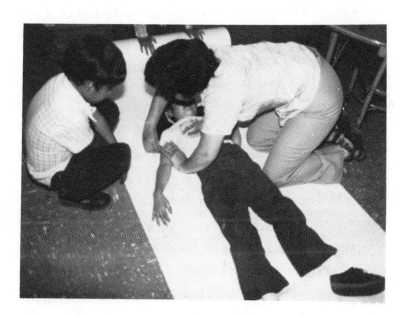

FEELING WORDS

PREPARATION:

Talk with your people about how words often evoke powerful feelings and images within us. Ask them to offer words that stand out in their own lives as being very important. Then have them describe their feelings while speaking or hearing these words.

IMAGERY:

Let's close our eyes and take a deep breath...very deep ... slowly taking in the air...filling our lungs with a sense of brightness ...lightness and peace...Breathe out now and use the power of your own breath to get rid of any tiredness...tension or distractions...negative thoughts...anything that might keep you from feeling totally at peace and at one within yourself(pause)... Take another deep breath...slowly drawing the air into your lungs...filling every cell in your body with a sense of your own power...your own lightness and brightness... and as you exhale, breathe out any tiredness...tension or distractions...negative thoughts...anything that might keep you from feeling totally at peace and at one within your-self(pause)...Now go deep within yourself...to a place that seems very dark yet very peaceful...that place in all of us where we experience a deep peace and sense of well being...Each of us has this wonderful center of quiet and peacefulness...and we can go here anytime we wish(pause)...While you are in this wonderfully quiet place...you will hear me say some words...They are im-portant words...and as you hear each one...allow your-self to receive an image that is related to the word...

to see something that represents the word in your life...
Take whatever images or symbols you get and be ready to
learn something from them...If by chance you don't receive any images for some of the words (or all of them)...
just enjoy the peacefulness within you...You'll be able
to do this exercise at another time...Get ready for
the first word...HAPPY!...What do you see when
you hear the word HAPPY?...What do you feel?...Do any
symbols come to you?(pause)...Now dismiss these images
and/or symbols and prepare yourself for the next word
...FEAR!...What do you see when you hear the word
FEAR?...What do you feel?...Do any symbols come to you?
(pause)...Now dismiss these images and/or symbols and
prepare yourself for the next word...SUCCESS! (Continue
in the same manner for FUTURE!...CAREER!...TRUST!...
LOVE!...SECURITY!...FRIENDSHIP!...)...Now go back over
the list and imprint on your mind the images and/or
symbols you received (Slowly repeat the words at this
time)...Do any of the words seem to affect you more
strongly than others?(pause)...Prepare yourself to return to us here in the room...fully alert...refreshed
and ready to work with the images...On the count of
three take a deep breath...exhale...and open your
eyes...One...two...

DISCUSSION:

Have your people talk about the images and/or symbols and
feelings they have for each word. Then ask them if the
images and/or symbols mean anything special to them.

SUPPLEMENTARY ACTIVITIES:

Art: Have your people draw their image/symbols for each word
on paper and include the written word on the page. Display
these around the room. Then have them identify others who
have similar symbols as theirs.

EXAMPLE:

Writing: Have your people identify the strongest or most preferred images and write compositions beginning with the word followed by the verb is.

EXAMPLE:

"HAPPY IS _____!"

FRIENDSHIP

PREPARATION:

Have your people discuss the meaning of friendship. Ask them to talk about the importance of friendship, the characteristics of a good friendship, how friends meet each other's needs and wants.

IMAGERY:

Picture yourself surrounded by some very good friends... These are very special people in your life...people whom you like to be with...people whom you trust...people with whom you can share your thoughts and feelings(pause)... Look at each friend...and as you do...see what makes this person so very special to you(pause)...Now look at all of your friends. Does any one person stand out among the rest?(pause)...If so, talk with this person and tell them how much you love being with them and how much you appreciate their friendship(pause)...Now listen to them tell you how you are so special to them(pause)... Prepare yourself to come back to us here in the room, refreshed and ready to work with this imagery...On the count of three...

DISCUSSION:

Whom did you see around you?

Did one special person stand out? If so, who?

What did you say to each other?

What makes these people (this one person) so very special to you?

What makes you so special to your friends?

Do you and your friends have special activities you like to do together? Certain places you like to visit?

"I used to chase lizards everyday after school with my friends."

Michael (Grade 9)

GETTING RID OF ANGER

PREPARATION:

Invite people to talk about anger: what it is, where they feel it in their bodies, what situations trigger anger, how they usually deal with anger.

IMAGERY: (PART I)

Travel inside your body until you come to the place where you hold (store) your anger(pause)... Look carefully at this place inside you...What does it look like? Do you see any people in there?...things?... colors?(pause)...Listen for voices...What do you hear?(pause)...Are there any smells at this place where you store anger?(pause)...Now think of a beautiful color that you like very much...Let this color wash over your anger. What happens to your anger when color washes over it?(pause)...Now let a scene that is very beautiful to you appear at the spot where you hold anger...What happens to your anger when the beautiful place takes over?(pause)...Now hear beautiful music and let this music fill this place...What happens to your anger when the beautiful music takes over?(pause)...Now check to see if any feelings of anger remain(pause)...If so, allow the color(s), beautiful scenery and music to completely take over your entire body...Relax and enjoy these comfortable feelings(pause)...Keep this feeling of peacefulness... stillness...calm...within you(pause)...On the count of three...

DISCUSSION:

Have your people discuss the questions posed in the imagery activity.

223

IMAGERY: (PART II)

Travel inside your body until you come to the place where you hold (store) your anger(pause)...Now picture a beautiful sun in the sky...It is friendly, warm, but not burning(pause)...Ask the sun to gently descend from the sky and let its light fall upon you... filling every cell in your body with its warmth... Feel that light penetrating your skin...muscles...even your bones(pause)...Now tell the light to travel to the spot where you hold your anger(pause)...Let the light mix with all the colors...images...feelings...sounds...smells of anger that you feel there(pause)...Now ask the sunlight to soak up the anger and to change it into soft, mellow, warm light for you(pause)...Notice how this feels...just letting the angry energy slowly change into beautiful warm sun energy. Do this until you feel all the anger is gone(pause)...Now take a deep breath...feel how light your body is at this time, how relaxed, how peaceful you feel(pause)...You can use this light to change anger or any other negative feelings any time you wish(pause)... Prepare yourself to return to us here in the room(pause) ...On the count of three...

DISCUSSION:

Describe how you felt while the sun was shining in your body.
What happened when the light soaked up your anger?
How do you feel now?

HAPPY MEMORIES

PREPARATION:

Tell your people that many medical professionals and psychologists believe that happy memories lead to both mental and physical health. It is good for us to recapture our own happy memories and to let these memories bring us joy in the present moment.

IMAGERY:

Close your eyes and take a deep breath...slowly breathe the air into your lungs, and as you do this, notice how you become lighter and lighter (pause)...As you breathe out, allow yourselves to feel a sense of floating...floating away from this place where we are now(pause)...Now take another deep breath...slowly filling your lungs with a sense of lightness and brightness...Hold it...Now exhale with a slight sigh and breathe out any tiredness...tension...or distractions you might be feeling at this time(pause)...Feel the peace within you...the sense of well being(pause) ...Now picture the sun...warm and shining in a wonderfully clear sky...and image yourself breathing in the liquid warmth from your sun...With each breath you take you feel the sun filling you with a wonderful light making you feel lighter and lighter...and brighter and brighter(pause)...Whenever you breathe out, remember to breathe out any tiredness...tension or distractions you might be feeling at this time (pause)...

At this time you are going to use your mind to travel back in time to a moment when you were very happy...a time when you were the happiest you can ever remember being...Everything was going well for you that day or that moment...Go there now and relive this happy moment...Experience this moment with all of your senses and feelings...as if this moment were happening right now...If by chance nothing comes to you at this time and you can't recall a happy moment...just remain calm within yourself and know that this moment may be your happiest moment...the moment that is best for you to remember...Whatever you are experiencing at this time is fine...Notice what's going on in this happy memory ...Are you alone or with others?...How are you feeling at this time?(pause)...Prepare yourself to return to us here in the room...fully alert...and refreshed... and ready to work with this imagery...On the count of three take a deep breath...hold it...and breathe out with a slight sigh while gently opening your eyes ...Keep this happy memory fresh in your mind and let it refresh you anytime you wish...One...two... three...

NOTE:

You might want your people to draw and/or paint their happy memories (and write about them) before discussing them with each other.

DISCUSSION:

Ask the following:

Describe your happiest moment(s). Where were you? What were you doing? Were others with you? What do you most remember about the moment(s)? What happens to your senses, your feelings in your body as you relive these happy memories right now? Are there certain parts of your body (i.e., head, shoulders, stomach, hands) that seem to remember your memories more than others?

SUPPLEMENTARY ACTIVITIES:

Art: Have your people draw and/or paint their memories. Make a large "happy memory" wall in the room where all of the happy memories can be displayed.

Writing: Have your people write a composition describing their happy memories. It is interesting when you have them do this in the first person "I" followed by present tense stream of consciousness.

"A long time ago when I was younger, I was at an elementary school. It was beautiful. There were some large trees and a large house in the center of the school grounds. There also was a teeter-totter in front of the large house. The house was white and had a red and blue roof. I was there with my friends. We used to play on the teeter-totter and jump rope. I was happy and everything was terrific."

Njat (Grade 10 - French II)

HAPPY THOUGHTS

PREPARATION:

Tell your people that in this imagery they will see, feel and experience happy thoughts. You might want to begin by asking them to share with each other thoughts that make them happy.

SUGGESTED MUSIC:

Golden Voyage, Vol. Two by Steve Halpern

IMAGERY:

Close your eyes and take a slow, deep breath...hold it... now exhale with a slight sigh(pause)...(Repeat as needed) ...Go away now to a beautiful place where you feel peaceful, relaxed...a place that makes you feel good all over (pause)...When you are there, take a moment to look at the scenery, listen to the sounds...notice any good smells.. feel some of the things that are pleasant to touch(pause) ...Now find a place to stretch out...a place where you can look into the sky and gently close your eyes, and as you do your mind becomes very quiet and your whole body seems very relaxed(pause)...Suddenly very happy thoughts start floating through your mind...and you feel great as you experience these thoughts...You have one minute of clock time which is all the time you need to experience these happy thoughts...So relax and enjoy them(Pause)...Now prepare yourself to come back to us in the room, fully alert, refreshed and ready to work with this imagery... One...two...three...

NOTE:

Before having your people discuss this imagery, you might want to give them crayons, colors or other drawing materials and have them draw and write about their happy thoughts.

DISCUSSION:

Describe the place where you had these happy thoughts.

What were your happy thoughts?

How did you feel (do you feel now) while having these happy thoughts?

Did any of the thoughts seem happier than others?

SUPPLEMENTARY ACTIVITIES:

Art: Have your people draw their happy thoughts. You might want them to cut out these thoughts and hang them around the room.

Writing: Have them write about their happy thoughts.
Describe your happy thought by becoming the thought and speaking (writing) in the first person.
What happy thoughts are in your mind right now?

Happy Thoughts

"I live in my house. I am happy. I am fifteen years old. I'm going to dance. I like to go to the beach. I like to ride my bicycle. My astrological sign is Scorpio. I like to eat at 12:00. I like chocolate, vanilla and strawberry ice cream. I have many friends."

Nancy (Grade 9 - Spanish I)

HEAVY FEELINGS

PREPARATION:

Ask people to talk about depression, how they feel, what their bodies look like when they are depressed. What do they do with their heads, shoulders, arms and hands when they are depressed? What happens to their voice? Then have them stand or sit, assume the body position that they usually find themselves in when depressed. Then ask them how others respond to them when they are depressed?

IMAGERY:

Travel away now to a place where you are alone...but safe...You are feeling depressed...at a low...burdened ...perhaps even confused...See what this feels like... You may notice a feeling of heaviness...tenseness coming over you(pause)...Exaggerate this feeling...be depressed and let the feelings be strong in you(pause)...Now somewhere in this place sit down and watch what thoughts come into your mind as you are experiencing depression ...What thoughts depress you?(pause)...While you are experiencing these depressing thoughts and feelings you suddenly notice a brilliant, friendly sun in the sky... The sun's rays feel so good...so warm...so comforting (pause)...Suddenly this wonderful sun begins to descend from the sky and slowly fills your entire body with its light...The light is soft and mellow and does not burn you(pause)...You begin to feel a tremendous warmth coming over you as the rays penetrate your skin...muscles...and even enter your bones ...The powerful sun is dissolving all the heavy, depressing energies and feelings you've been experiencing(pause)...These heavy feelings are absorbed into the sun's magnificent light and warmth... and as this happens you notice that all the depressing

230

thoughts begin to leave your mind...and are replaced by joyful, happy ones(pause)...Your body feels lighter and lighter. Your feelings become lighter and lighter(pause)... ...Your depression is replaced by joy. Notice the joyful thoughts that accompany these feelings...Let these joyful thoughts flood your mind(pause)...At this time you notice the sun once again ascending to its place in the sky... leaving you feeling light-hearted...happy...warm(pause)... Remember, you can change your feelings or your mood anytime you wish by calling upon the sun's light and warmth, and your positive thoughts to help you ...Prepare yourself now to return to us here in the room...fully refreshed.. and ready to work with your experiences(pause)... On the count of three...

DISCUSSION:

Describe in detail what feelings you experienced while the sun was shining in and through you.

What body sensations did you notice?

How are you feeling now?

SUPPLEMENTARY ACTIVITIES:

Art: Have your people draw and/or make a huge sun to hang in the room. This sun will be used as a symbol for lightening up - for taking away depressed feelings.

Have your children make feeling masks to show how they feel for the day.

Movement: Have your people do movement (dance) to celebrate their good feelings - their lightheartedness.

"My mommy is in
the hospital and
her stomach hurts.
I miss her very
much."
Rosa (Kindergarten)

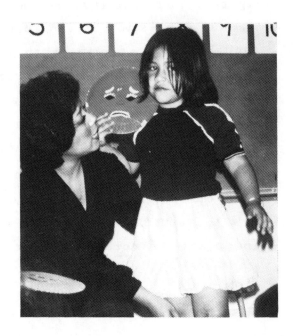

'Today after school, my brother is going to take me to a
soccer game."   Tom (Grade 1)

I AM NOT MY PROBLEMS

PREPARATION:

We often identify with our problems instead of seeing the problems as separate from ourselves. Have your people write the following: "I have problems, but I am not my problems." Then direct them to draw or sketch themselves as strong, centered, and able to handle any problems that come their way. They write their problems around this figure of themselves, symbolizing that the problems exist separate from them. Then they repeat (or write) for each one: "I have a problem with _____ (i.e., worrying too much), but I am not this problem."

MATERIALS:

Colored pens, crayons, markers and paper.

IMAGERY:

Close your eyes...take a deep breath...let it out... As you do this feel your body becoming more and more relaxed(pause)...Take another deep breath...let it out ...as you do this feel your body becoming more relaxed (pause)...Go away now to a place where everything seems quite beautiful...a place where you feel good(pause)... While you are there sit down and relax a moment...just looking around and taking everything in(pause)...Now somewhere in your picture see a double of you...a mirror image of yourself...your alter ego(pause)...Around this image you see all your problems...all the concerns that weigh you down...These concerns are floating around you (pause)...Notice how they float around you...and you aren't caught up in them(pause)...Picture yourself as centered...strong...in command of them(pause)...You have problems but you are not your problems...Say that to yourself..."I have problems but I am not my problems... and my problems are not me"(pause)...Say this again... "I have problems but I am not my problems...and my problems are not me"(pause)...As you see these problems floating around you...reach out and take each one in your hand...hold it...examine it...and feel how much power you have to control it...to change it(pause)...Now take each problem in your hand and change it into something helpful for you...Do this for each problem(pause)...Now see your-self with all these changed forms...energies...floating around you...You have done this with your own creative power(pause)...Prepare yourself to return to us here in the room...On the count of three take a deep breath... exhale...and slowly open your eyes...alert and ready to work with this experience(pause)...Take a few moments to re-do your drawing from before the imagery, and see if you add any new information.

DISCUSSION:

What problems did you see floating around you?
How did you change them?
What did you learn about yourself by doing this?

SUPPLEMENTARY ACTIVITIES:

Art: Have your people make large posters based on their experiences and post these around the room.

Drama: Each person decides which problems seem to be the most pressing. Others in the group are chosen as "alter egos" for these problems and dialogue with the person having the problems.

EXAMPLE:

Person: "Getting into a good college and personal satisfaction are my main concerns at this time."

(Two people volunteer to act as "College" and "Satisfaction".)

College: "Study hard and you'll be accepted by me. Keep visualizing yourself as a successful student."

Satisfaction: "If you always do what feels right in your heart, and have the interests of others at heart, you'll feel good about your life."

Person: "What if I study hard but study all the wrong things for the tests?"

College: "Don't worry! This won't happen."

I AM UNIQUE

PREPARATION:

Ask your people to list some of their personality characteristics such as "loyal", "calm", "pensive", "excitable", and the like. Then ask them to think about their unique qualities... those things that make them special in the world. You might have group members call out qualities for each other.

IMAGERY:

Imagine that you have just been born. Family members are looking at you with great love and admiration(pause)... They don't know it but you can see them looking at you. You feel their love, care, excitement. They are wondering what you'll be like(pause)...In your mind you know what you'll be like for you know everything about yourself, your strengths, likes, talents, ideas, feelings... You have one minute of clock time which is all the time you need to experience yourself just being born and knowing everything about yourself...Use this time to see what you are like(pause)...Now look at yourself today...You've begun to develop some of these strengths, likes, talents, ideas, feelings...What are you like today?(pause)...Now picture yourself alone...by yourself...but feeling peaceful... quiet...centered(pause)...Soon someone comes up to you who seems to know you quite well(pause)...Suddenly this person begins telling you how very special you are... how really unique you are...Perhaps they even tell you how the world needs you...your gifts...your inspiration...your love...You have 30 seconds of clock time which is all the time you need to experience this person(pause)...On the count of three take a slow...deep breath...

236

DISCUSSION:

Describe the scene where you where looking at your family.

What were they saying about you?

What thoughts did you have about yourself at this time? What strengths...likes...preferences...talents...ideas...feelings did you recognize?

Which ones seem strongest in your life today?

SUPPLEMENTARY ACTIVITIES:

Writing: Have your people write a short composition beginning with "I am a person who_____." Have them use verbs such as "is", "wants", "likes", "is good at", "knows about", "helps others", etc. as focusers for their descriptions.

Art: Have your people draw themselves and cut these out. Then have them select key words that describe how they are and hang these words from their body cutouts. Then the cutouts with words are hung as mobiles.

Have them draw cartoons of themselves as unique persons, and write third person descriptions of their uniqueness.

"I am a person who:

... is so smart

... likes to dance

... has problems

... wants to be better

... knows everybody

... believes in God

... hopes to be a doctor

... dreams everyday

... needs a lot of help"

Gary (Grade 9)

I Am Unique

I'm the space
  a place
  for miracles and dreams.
A place
  to explore
  more
  life.
A place
  for wonders.
A mystery in itself.
A creation
  with a conscience.
A place
  for stars and dream planets.
A place to be
  the space.

Kim (Grade 6)

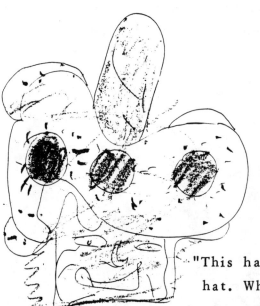

"This happy man always wears a flashing light hat. Wherever he goes, people look upon him as a totally insane person. But within himself he knows that he is different and unique. By wearing this strange hat, it shows how he sees himself, not how other people see him."

Tom (Grade 10)

238

IMPORTANT PERSONS THAT HELP ME

PREPARATION:

Discuss the meaning of friendship with your people. Ask
them to talk about how friends help them, make them feel good,
and how friends help each other grow strong and happy in
their lives. Have them talk about friends within their own
family as well as friends in their extended families.

IMAGERY:

Go away to a wonderful place where you feel calm...
relaxed(pause)...Look around and notice the many
beautiful things that are in this place(pause)...Feel
a deep sense of joy that this place is within you and
that you can come here anytime you wish(pause)...Very
soon one or more special persons will come visit you.
These are important people in your life, people who know
and love you and are willing to help you any in way they
can. Look around, now, and see who these people are...
If someone comes whom you don't recognize, know that
you may be seeing someone you will meet soon ... Ask
this important person (or these important persons)
to sit down near you and ask each one the following
question: "Why am I so special to you?"...and then
wait for the person to answer. If you don't receive
an answer, it means you are not supposed to receive an
answer at this time. You will receive an answer when
you are ready(pause)...Now tell each person how much
you care for them...how they are so very special to you
(pause)...When this is finished, ask each person if they
have any advice to offer you at this time(pause)...Finish
this conversation and prepare to come back to us here in
the room, refreshed and ready to work with your experiences...On the count of three...

SUPPLEMENTARY ACTIVITIES:

Art: Have people draw and or paint this experience.

Drama: Work in groups to role play the situation. One person volunteers to read his/her "Important Person" and chooses others to be these persons. These surrogate "Important Persons" then approach the individual and say appreciative things to him/her.

EXAMPLE:

#1) Marcie (Reads account of the experience involving her dad, uncle and her friend, Terry.)

#2) (Dad): "Marcie, I love you. You are very special."

#3) (Uncle): "You've got a great spirit and you make everyone feel good."

#4) (Terry): "You're just great to be with."

I asked God to help me and she did.

Wendy (Grade 8)

240

"I saw my dad, my sister Lynn, my friend Auggie and my Aunt. Dad said he loved me because I was his son and that he felt very close to me. Lynn said I was special to her because we share everything with each other. We're always very open. Auggie told me I'm a really good soccer player and he admires my talent. My Aunt said she's always felt very close to me because when I was little, I used to sit on her lap and have her tell me stories!

I told my dad that he's always been very fair with me and I think he's very wise. The other kids admire him too. I told Lynn that she always builds me up - especially when I'm down. I told Auggie that he helps me feel good about myself. I told my Aunt that she always seems to be there for me, especially when I need to talk things over with someone who loves me but can be objective."

Peter (Grade 10)

A JOYFUL PLACE TO BE

PREPARATION:

Have your people talk about the feeling called "joy". Ask them to describe when they feel joyful. What are they doing? Where are they? Are they with someone special? What memories bring them joy?

IMAGERY:

Travel away to a place where you feel great joy. When you arrive at this place...take time to look around and experience it with all of your senses...observe...listen... touch...feel...smell...taste(pause)...What makes this be a place of such joy for you? How is it special to you? (pause)...What things in this place make you feel joy- ful?(pause)...Are there people here who bring you joy? (pause)...Are there smells...textures...foods...other items that bring you joy?...You have one minute of clock time which is all the time you need to experience your feelings of joy(pause)...On the count of three...

DISCUSSION:

Where did you go? What did you see?...hear?...touch?...feel? smell?...taste?

Who was there with you, if anyone?

How does your body feel when you feel joy?

SUPPLEMENTARY ACTIVITIES:

Poetry: Have your people write poems beginning with the word "Joy".

Art: Have your people make murals of their places of joy.

242

VARIATION 1:

Replace the word "joy" with other feeling words you might wish your people to experience such as "trust", "security", "acceptance", "love" , "wisdom", "intelligence", etc.

VARIATION 2:

Have your students who are in a foreign language class write of their joyful place in the target language.

A La Montagne

Je suis à la montagne avec ma famille. Nous grimpons au sommet de la montagne. Je me sens heureuse. Mes parents ne sont pas heureux parce qu'ils n'aiment pas grimper au sommet de la montagne.

"I am in the desert with my friends and my family. The desert is hot. My friends and I are taking a walk in the desert. I am happy. My friends and my family are happy also."

Sharon (Grade 9 - French I)

LEARNING ABOUT MYSELF THROUGH PROJECTION: TREE

PREPARATION:

None is needed for these exercises. It is better to let your people fully experience their projections, and then discuss possible meanings and interpretations after the imageries have been completed.

IMAGERY:

Go away now to a place where you find beautiful trees, flowers, animals...a place where you feel refreshed...
...calm...secure...mellow...happy(pause)...Look around and carefully note everything in your environment...What do you see?...hear?...feel?...
...touch?...smell?...taste?(pause)...Are you alone or with others?(pause)...How do you feel within yourself at this time?(pause)...Look around once again and find a tree...a tree that seems very special to you...a tree that attracts you to look more closely at it(pause)...Examine the tree carefully and notice everything about the tree...trunk...bark... branches...leaves...height(pause)...See if there is fruit on the tree(pause)...flowers(pause)...birds or other animals on the branches(pause)...How large is the trunk? the branches?the leaves?(pause)...Now back away from your tree until you can see the whole tree in front of you...Begin describing the tree to itself by saying "Tree, you are _____." (Use whatever words and phrases you need to adequately describe the tree such as "Tree, you are tall, slender and you seem very graceful. When the wind blows through your leaves you remind me of a ballet dancer moving gently across the

stage.")(pause)...Now continue your description by adding this next part that also describes you... "Tree, you are ____ and I am ____ " and continue describing yourself in relation to the Tree. Just let your feelings and ideas flow...Accept whatever you say as true for you on some level(pause)...Complete this dialogue and prepare to return to us here in the room... fully refreshed and ready to work with these experiences (pause)...On the count of three...

DISCUSSION:

Following the imagery have your people draw their trees and write brief summaries of how they described their trees trees and how they described themselves in relation to their trees.

EXAMPLE:

"Tree you are very strong and rooted deep in the ground. I am strong and people can depend on me, too. You have thick branches and I am a solid person. You can hold animals, kids, and fruit on your strong branches and I can too."

                                        Karl (Grade 11)

When descriptions are completed, ask each person to tell you what they've learned about themselves in doing this projection exercise. You may invite the others to give feedback if you feel there is a strong sense of camaraderie, trust and overall friendship within the group.

EXAMPLE:

L. Have you learned anything about yourself from this projection exercise?

S. Yes, I always feel strong and able to help others. I'm also very practical and don't tend to get carried away by my feelings and ideas. I stay balanced and that's why I think I'm a good leader-type person.

VARIATION:

Have people work with a partner or in small groups. One

person shows his/her drawing to the others, and the others talk to the drawing, describing it. The person who owns the drawing listens to these descriptions and sees if anything that is said relates to him or her.

EXAMPLE: (Two people working together)

#1   (Shows drawing)

#2   (Talking to the drawing)

   Tree, you are huge, tall and graceful. You reach to the sky. In fact most of your branches are very high, away from the ground.

#1   (Responding to the description)

   I spend a lot of time in my head and I often feel far away from people around me, especially when I'm thinking about various ideas. When I'm not doing serious thinking, I feel more like I want to be around people.

VARIATION:

   Suggest other items such as flowers, lakes, oceans, houses, and cars as other possibilities for projection.

_____

"I am a tree. I am tall and full of leaves. I look like a tall lady with frizzy hair. When I was just a seed, I wanted to be big and lovely like other trees around me. When the rains came, I felt cold and wet. I wanted the sun to come out and give me warmth and dry me up.

Then, one day when the sun was out, a man came along with a chainsaw and cut me down. As the saw cut into my trunk, I felt a deep burning pain, and I knew I wasn't going to live long.

When I fell over, I fell on top of the little trees around me and killed them all. It wasn't my fault. The lumberjacks should have known that would happen. Then I was stacked on a logging truck with other trees. I felt sad leaving my home in the forest.

The truck bounced over the road and I couldn't wave goodbye, because they chopped my arms off. The last thing I remember was the peaceful quietness of the forest."

                                        Vicky (Grade 10)

246

Andrew (Grade 3) drew this tree and made these comments <u>before</u> doing the above guided imagery ...

"This is my tree. I like climbing trees and being alone in the sunshine reading under my tree."

Andrew's tree and comments as a result of the guided imagery activity ...

"I feel happy when I am a tree and when the apples and leaves grow on me. My tree talked to me and said he wished he was like me so that he could run around and talk and ask questions, and sit under him and read."

NOTE: Because of his disruptive behavior both at home and at school, Andrew was placed in a learning disabled class, and is receiving adjunct intensive personal therapy. The therapist working with him found this type of imagery projection activity extremely helpful in assisting Andrew to verbalize his frustrations and feelings.

LIGHTENING UP

PREPARATION:

Ask your people to tell you what they do to help themselves feel better when they are feeling depressed. Do they talk with others? Go off by themselves? Read poetry? Visit a certain place? Ask them to describe how what they do makes them feel better, feel lighter, less depressed. Then suggest to them that they can "lighten up" (get rid of depressed feelings) by creating a pleasant scene in their minds.

IMAGERY:

Now go away to a place, person or situation that makes you feel good(pause)...If you are with a person, talk with them...be with them as you usually are...Experience their good energy around you... Watch what happens to you when you do this(pause)...If you are not with someone at this time, then see yourself being in a special place that makes you feel good...Perhaps you're in your room listening to certain songs...dancing...playing the guitar... reading poetry or a good book...Or maybe you find yourself outside playing sports...walking in nature...You know what's best for you...you know how to make yourself feel better...Do this now and watch what happens to your feelings as you do this(pause)...Continue creating this scene in your mind until you feel better, lighter, happier (pause)...Now on the count of three take a deep breath...

DISCUSSION:

Who (or what place) did you call into your imagery?
Describe your feelings while being with this person (or at

this place).

How do you feel now after just completing this imagery activity?

SUPPLEMENTARY ACTIVITY:

Art: Have people draw themselves with their special person (or in a special place) and show what positive feelings emerge at this time.

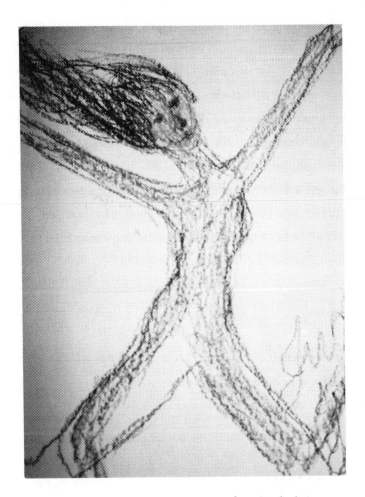

Judy (Adult)

LONELINESS

PREPARATION:

Discuss the meaning of loneliness. Ask your people to talk about times when they have felt lonely...what they did about their loneliness, what they learned from it.

IMAGERY:

Picture yourself all alone, feeling lonely(pause)...Where are you?(pause)...What are you doing?(pause)...What's happening around you?(pause_...Allow all of your feelings of loneliness to surface and feel them intensely(pause) While you are experiencing your aloneness, you will have an insight about yourself, something you can learn about you and/or others...What can loneliness teach you at this time? You have one minute of clock time which is all the time you need to learn from your experience with loneliness(pause)...Prepare yourself to return to us here in the room fully refreshed and ready to work with this imagery ...On the count of three...

DISCUSSION:

Describe your feelings of loneliness. Was there (is there) a difference between being alone and being lonely?
What did you learn about yourself and/or others?

SUPPLEMENTARY ACTIVITIES:

Poetry: Have your people write poems about their feelings.

The Lonely Girl

Once there was a girl named Lisa.
She had just moved to Portland, Oregon
from Mexico. All the children where she
lived made fun of her because of her
hat. It was a hat her grandmother had
given her and it was very special to
her, but they did not know that. They
hurt her feelings very badly. Lisa
would cry every night because of how
mean the other children were to her.
But she refused to leave her hat at
home. So she never talked to the kids
at school. They did not call her Lisa.
They called her "Lonely Girl".

                    Lisa (Grade 10)

LOOKING AHEAD

PREPARATION:

Tell your people that they will use this imagery exercise to imagine themselves in the future. They will notice what they are doing and what they did to get there.

IMAGERY:

Close your eyes...breathe deeply...follow your breath...relax your body(pause)...Now see yourself five years from now(pause)...Notice what you look like...where you live...what you are doing(pause) ...Are you happy?...satisfied?...Are you going to school?...working?...Notice your responsibilities (pause)...Now take one minute of clocktime equal to all of the time that you need to notice what steps you took to get here(pause)...Now bring yourself back to present time and remember everything you have learned about yourself(pause) ...When you are ready, open your eyes(pause)... Let's discuss our experiences.

DISCUSSION:

Describe in detail what you were doing five years from now. Include where you live and work, how you play, etc.

Name important persons in your life at this time.

What steps did you take to get from your present situation to the one five years from now?

Are you happy (satisfied) with what you saw yourself doing five years from now? If not, what steps can you take now to change your future?

"I will be a secret agent or a rock singer or an engineer. I will buy a house near the beach and I will buy a truck and a camper and travel all over the USA. I will go to France, Hong Kong and Mexico. I will have a radio and a television and I will buy a boat."

Frank (Grade 9 - French I)

LOVE

PREPARATION:

Have your people discuss love, what it means, and how they
experience it in their lives.

IMAGERY:

In this imagery we are going to meet LOVE. Go away now
to a place that is beautiful, special, wonderful to you
...Look around and take in the beauty that you see...
and listen to the marvelous sounds at this special place
(pause)...If you'd like, reach out and touch some of the
things in this beautiful place(pause)...Perhaps there is
something there you can smell or taste(pause)...Now find
a place to sit down, if you are not already sitting
down...and in a moment you will meet LOVE(pause)...
Close your eyes in this place and take a slow...deep
breath...and as you exhale, LOVE will come to you at this
place...Open your eyes and look around until you see
LOVE...Don't place any expectations on what LOVE will
look and feel like...Take whatever you get...If by chance
nothing comes to you at this time...then enjoy the quiet
within you and know that you will receive your image of
LOVE at another time when you are ready...You have one
minute of clock time which is all the time you need to
experience LOVE (pause)...If you'd like, ask love any
questions you wish to know about yourself, your life,
other people. Give LOVE a voice and let LOVE answer your
questions(pause)...Prepare yourself now to return to
us here in the room...fully alert and refreshed...ready
to work with this imagery...On the count of three...

DISCUSSION:

Describe how you met LOVE. What form did LOVE take? What question(s) did you ask LOVE? What answers did you receive?

VARIATION:

Replace the word "love" with other feeling words you might wish your people to experience such as "joy", "happiness", "trust", "appreciation", "wisdom", and the like.

SUPPLEMENTARY ACTIVITIES:

Poetry: Have your people write poems about love.

"Love is looking at a beautiful sunset with a good friend."

Peter (Grade 10)

LOVE CIRCLE

PREPARATION:

Discuss the concept of love as good energy that flows within our bodies keeping us healthy, and also flows between and among people, keeping us healthy. Mention the importance of working together in love and closeness with one another.

IMAGERY:

Close your eyes...Imagine you are looking at the sun... Let your sun be beautiful and warm...Notice how your sun seems very friendly and does not burn you(pause)...Let the sun come to the top of your head and begin to descend through your body...Let the sun go through your whole body until it exits through the bottom of your feet into the ground beneath you. You have one minute to do this(pause)...Now open your eyes and look at everyone in the room(pause)...Look at your hands and see the light in your hands(pause)...Take your light and toss it into the center of the room for everyone to share...Notice how you receive the same light from everyone else(pause)...Now think about someone whom you love very much...Let them be in the center of this room receiving the same light as you(pause)...Now make a wish that we all become more lovable and happy...See everyone very happy and filled with love(pause)...Let's get into a circle and hold hands. Put love and happiness in your hands and send them to the person on your right...Then receive love and happiness from the person on your left...We'll pass love and happiness around the room(pause)...While we are doing this tell me what you see and feel...

Student 1: I feel very light and warm. I see lots of

colors.

Student 2: I feel good.

Student 3: I feel bright and warm.

VARIATION:

If there are any negative feelings in the group such as anger, jealousy, hurt or illness of any kind (i.e., cold, flu, stomach ache, headaches, serious illnesses such as cancer, leukemia) have the group form a straight line with a trash can or waste container at one end. The group images their most positive, loving and healthy thoughts pushing out the negativity into the trash can. The trash can is then dumped as a symbol of the triumph of good feelings over negative ones.

NOTE:

If you have people with life threatening illnesses such as cancer or leukemia, do not promise that this activity will rid them of the disease. The idea is to draw upon the life force (love energies) of the entire group to help the person feel supported by others. Sometimes this leads to physical healing.

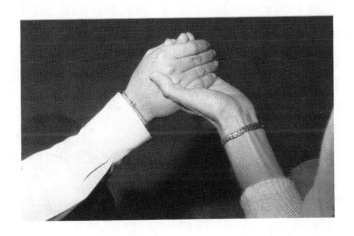

MEETING OUR FEARS

PREPARATION:

Have your people talk about things they fear the most.
Discuss ways of handling fear...ways of overcoming fear.
Perhaps some of your people can tell stories about
themselves or others that describe times of overcoming
fear.

IMAGERY:

Close your eyes and take a slow...deep breath...
hold it...now exhale with a slight sigh(pause)...
(Repeat as needed)...Go away to a deep green forest
that has many trees, bushes, leaves, rocks and some
water(pause)...When you look up, you can see the sun
shining through the leaves of the trees(pause)...
(pause)...As you walk through the forest you see
a small cabin-like house(pause)...Inside this
cabin live your fears...Walk up to the cabin
and stand in front of it(pause)...Surround
yourself with a beautiful golden white light...
This is the light of your inner wisdom and
intelligence...and it will protect you from any
harm(pause)...If you need to...ask someone to come
and stand beside you...someone who will help to
protect you from your fears...someone who will
help you overcome them(pause)...Call out to
your fears and ask them to open the door and come
out in the light so you can see them...They may appear
as symbols...animals...other people...so take whatever
you get(pause)...Look around you and find a magic
wand or stick...You will use this wand to change your

fears into something helpful for you(pause)...
Now go up to each fear and tell it that you are in
control of your life and that you do not wish to
live with it in you anymore...And as soon as you
have talked with it...take your magic wand and
touch the fear and watch it change into something
helpful for you...You have one minute of clock time
which is all the time you need to change your fears
(pause)...Prepare yourself now to return to us here
in the room...fully alert...refreshed and ready to
work with this imagery...One...

DISCUSSION:

What were your fears?

How did they appear in your imagery? Were they symbols?
animals? people?

What did you say to your fears? Did your fears say anything
to you?

When you touched them with your magic wand, what happened
to them?

Did you call upon a guide to help you? If so, what part did
the guide play in helping you to change your fears?

SUPPLEMENTARY ACTIVITIES:

Art: Have your people draw their fears being changed by
their magic wand.

Writing: Have them write a short story depicting how they
were able to change their fears.

Drama: Select others to role play various fears and have
each person do a drama dance around these "fears",
demonstrating the person's power to overcome their fears.

259

"I don't fear my leukemia anymore, because I know
I can call on Magic Pac-Man to gobble all the bad
cells up and get them all out of my body."
                              Larry (Grade 8)

NEEDS AND WANTS

PREPARATION:

Discuss the idea of basic needs - things your people need for survival, pleasure, career, school, etc.

IMAGERY:

Imagine yourself walking through a beautiful green forest. The day is lovely. There is much sun and warmth in the sky(pause)...Nature seems very mellow, today, leaving you with an overall feeling of well being(pause)...As you walk along, you notice a large box in the center of the road, so you stop and look at it(pause)...Somewhere on the box you find your name and a note that says "Needs and Wants"(pause)...You decide to look inside the box to see what is there(pause)...Whatever you find is symbolic of your needs and wants at this time...Don't worry if you are not able to immediately understand the meaning of what you find inside the box(pause)...Now give your symbol(s) a voice and ask it to tell you what it means to you... You have one minute of clock time which is all the time you need to experience this(pause)...Prepare yourself to return to us here in the room and work with this imagery...On the count of three...

DISCUSSION:

Describe the place where you walked. Were there trees? flowers? animals? other people? What did your box look like?
What was inside?
What do these symbols (does this symbol) mean to you?
What did your symbols (symbol) say to you?

261

SUPPLEMENTARY ACTIVITIES:

Art: Have your people draw or make these boxes including the item(s) found inside.

Have them draw or make only their symbols and label them with descriptions of what the symbols mean.

Writing: Have them write short compositions beginning with the statement:"Right now in my life I need_____." or "Right now in my life I want_____." After they have listed their needs and/or wants, you might ask them to come up with a statement that shows how they will fulfill their needs and wants such as "I need more appreciation from my dad and when it feels right, I'm going to tell him I need him to spend more time with me."

NOTE: You might have your people talk about the differences between needs and wants, with needs being stronger. Then have them reexamine their list and indicate which are needs and which are wants.

PAINT WITH LOVE

PREPARATION:

Have your people discuss the meaning of love, and ways in which we show our love to others, such as hugging, kissing, holding hands, giving and receiving gifts, spending time together, sending letters. Then show them your hands and have them look at their hands. Tell them to imagine a color of love spreading all over your and their hands. You and they are going to show each other how much you love and care for each other by painting each other with the color of love. We suggest you begin by painting a few people with your love. Once your people are comfortable with the activity, you invite them to do so with each other.

SUGGESTED MUSIC:

Pachelbel Kanon by James Galway; You Are So Beautiful To Me by Joe Cocker; The First Time Ever I Saw Your Face by Roberta Flack.

IMAGERY:

Rub your hands together and feel how warm they become as you do this(pause)...As you are rubbing them together, think how much love you have in your heart(pause)... Stop rubbing your hands...and let them rest quietly in front of you(pause)...Be aware of how your hands feel at this time...Are they warm?...tingling?...full of energy?(pause)...Now take the love in your heart and send it down your arms to your hands(pause)...Feel this love in your hands(pause)...See a color of love around your hands(pause)...Open your eyes now, and find a partner(pause)...One of you will go first...so decide

263

this now(pause) (For younger children you might wish to decide who will go first.) Start at the top of the head... move your hands down both sides of the person's body, moving from the head...past the ears...jaws...neck.. shoulders...arms...hands...hips...legs...knees...feet... While you are doing this, send your partner thoughts of love. See him or her covered with your color of love... (pause)...(For younger children you might wish to allow 30 seconds for this. For older children or adults, we allow one to five minutes per person, depending on the degree of intensity we wish to create.)...Now the person who has been receiving the love prepare yourself to be the giver...(repeat from "Start at the top of the head ...")

NOTE:

You may wish to have the group divide up into partners before you start the imagery, rather than having them find a partner in the midst of the imagery, especially if you are working with a younger or less self-directed group. Also, you may wish to have your people paint several others in the group.

NOTE:

We suggest that you lead this imagery at least once a week during a special "love time". You might want to begin by painting a few people with your love and then inviting them to do this with each other.

DISCUSSION:

How did you feel while being painted?

How did you feel while painting your partner?

Did you see or feel the color being sent by your partner?

Did you notice any sensations in your hands while you were doing the painting?

What loving thoughts did you have about your partner?

Would you like to tell them these thoughts?

ART:

Paint a picture of the person whom you painted with love.
Draw your partner surrounded by your color of love.
Cut it out and place on a special bulletin board.

VARIATION:

Have your people close their eyes and picture someone whom
they love very much. **They image themselves painting**
this special person with love, and then they see themselves
being painted by this person.

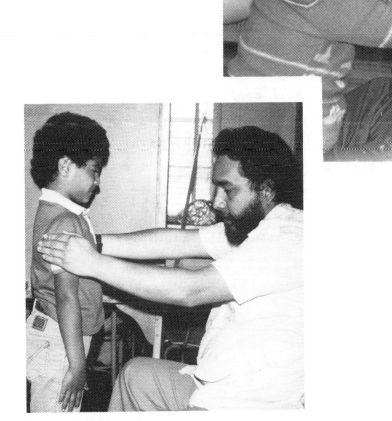

PASSING TESTS

PREPARATION:

It is best that your people have worked with the "Successful Me" imagery so that they understand the relationship between inner imagery and physical performance. You then mention that they can use the same skill for passing exams.

IMAGERY:

Take a long...deep breath...and exhale any tension you are feeling at this time...Let it all out(pause) ...Do this again and release any tension you might be experiencing(pause)...This imagery will help us do well on our test...Take another long...deep breath ...and exhale any doubts you have about your ability to do well on the test(pause)...Now picture yourself taking the test...confident...prepared...knowing the answers...convinced you will do well(pause)...Now picture yourself...pencil or pen in hand...writing the answers (or if the test is oral verbalizing the answers to the examiner)...knowing all of them(pause) ...You feel so relaxed...so confident taking this test(pause)...Now see yourself finishing the test... opening your eyes...and handing the test in to be scored...A little while later you receive the results and you did very well...See how well you did(pause)... Whenever you take any test keep this image in your mind ...the image of your doing very well on the test(pause) ...On the count of three...

NOTE:

Following the imagery, have your people repeat to themselves: "I did very well on this test."

PROBLEM SOLVING

PREPARATION:

Talk with your people about their own inner wisdom, their
ability to direct their own lives and to solve their own
problems. Sometimes problem solving requires assistance
from others, but nevertheless it is we ourselves who,
by contacting the wisdom within us, ultimately direct
our own lives.

IMAGERY:

Let's take a deep breath...and go inside ourselves to
that place of peace and oneness...And as we breathe
out we rid ourselves of any tiredness...tension...
distractions...anything that would keep us from being
totally at one and at peace within ourselves(pause)
...Now think of a problem that you are experiencing
at this time in your life...See the problem appearing before you...It may be a person...situation...
place...thing(pause)...Now look around and find a box
large enough to hold the entire problem(pause)...Put
your problem in this box...Don't worry about the problem being too heavy for the box...If it is too heavy,
just make your box strong enough to hold it(pause)
...Close the box...pick it up...and find yourself a
road and begin walking down your road while carrying your box...If the box is too heavy for you, create
someone or thing to help you with it(pause)...As you
walk along, notice the scenery...the weather...other
people, if others are there with you(pause)...Now
look up ahead and notice a rather tall mountain
and begin walking up this mountain...all the way to

267

the top...If you need help getting to the top with
your heavy problem box...then create something like
a magic wand...wagon or a strong person to help you
with it(pause)...When you arrive at the top...stop
and rest a moment...Close your eyes and let relaxation
flow throughout your body...calming every nerve...
every muscle...Remember to take some deep breaths to
help you relax(pause)...Suddenly you see a very wise
person who has the answer or answers to your problem...Take a close look at this person and see if you
recognize him or her(pause)...Now open your box and
show your very wise person your problem...This
person is all loving...caring...understanding and
will tell you whatever you need to know to deal
with this problem, so listen carefully to whatever
he or she says...You have one minute of clocktime
which is all the time you need to talk with your
wise person(pause)...Before ending your discussion
ask your wise person any other questions you need
to better understand anything he or she said...
And know that it is OK if you still don't understand the full meaning of everything the person
said to you...Full understanding may come later
(pause)...Thank the person for their help...pick
up your box...and notice if it feels any lighter
(pause)...Walk down your mountain...to the road
...and continue walking down your road feeling
how nice it is to know that you have within you
the answers to your problems...Anytime you want
to resolve a problem you can go within yourself to
your place of peace and quiet...and consult your
own wise person(pause)...Take a deep breath...
hold it...and exhale with a slight sigh...feeling
the lightness and brightness within you(pause)...
On the count of three take another deep breath...
and prepare yourself to return to us here in the

room...fully alert and refreshed...and ready to
work with this imagery...One...two...

NOTE:

You might want your people to draw and write about their
experiences before discussing them.

DISCUSSION:

Describe your problem. What did you put in your box?
Describe your road and your journey to the top of the
mountain. Did you need help to carry the box? If
so what kind of help did you create?
Describe your wise person. Did you recognize the person?
What advice did the person give you?
Did you ask your wise person any questions? If so what
did you ask?

SUPPLEMENTARY ACTIVITIES:

Art: Have your people draw and/or paint their boxes with the
problem(s) inside.
Have them draw and/or paint their meeting with the
wise person.
Writing: Have them write compositions describing their experiences. You might want them to write on the drawings.
Drama: Have your people work as partners and role play
the dialogue between the individual and his/her own
wise person. One partner is the wise person and the
other is the seeker.

REVIEWING MY LIFE

PREPARATION:

Have your people discuss major events, highlights, important turning points in their lives. Then lead them in this imagery activity to relive these moments.

IMAGERY:

Close you eyes and focus your attention on your breath(pause)...See yourself as you are now... and notice all of the aspects of your life... Notice your family...your friends...your home...your activities...your clothes...your food...how you feel about yourself(pause)... Now we are going to move back in time 5 years and notice all the aspects of your life 5 years ago(pause)(Repeat family...friends...home, etc.) ...Now move back in time another 5 years and notice what's happening at this time. (pause)... Notice your family...your friends...your activities ...your clothes...your food...Pay special attention to how you are feeling about yourself(pause)...Are there certain things you like to do?(pause)... (Depending on the age of the students, move back in time another 5 years.) Prepare yourself to come back to us here in the room...When I count to three... slowly open your eyes...remembering the important aspects of your life...and begin to write your autobiography...One...two...three...

DISCUSSION:

Where were you and what were you doing five years ago...

ten years ago?

Who were your friends?

What were your hobbies?

What clothes were you wearing? What foods were you eating?

How were you feeling about yourself then?

Were there certain things you liked to do then?

SUPPLEMENTARY ACTIVITY:

Art: Have your people make posters illustrating important
events in their lives. Give them blank transparencies and
have them draw these events on the transparencies. They then
show these as "films" to the others, who try to guess what
each important event was.

QUAND J'ÉTAIS PETIT, J'AVAIS UNE
BALLE, J'AVAIS UNE BICYCLETTE, DES
PATINS, ET UN "KICK & GO". J'AVAIS UN
CHIEN ET J'ENSEIGNAIS À MON CHIEN
À SE TENIR TRANQUIL ET À SE
TENIR DEBOUT.

"When I was little, I had a ball, a bicycle, some
skates and a skateboard. I had a dog and I taught
him to be quiet and to stand up."

Paul (Grade 10- French II)

271

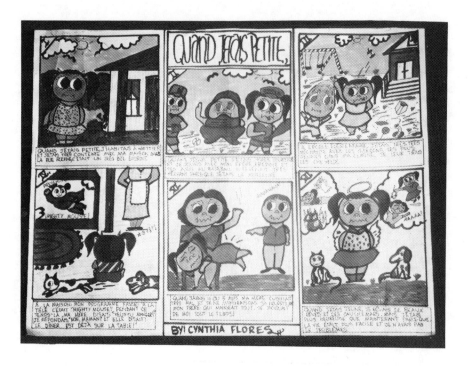

"When I was little, we used to live in Whittier and I was very happy there in my house on Rockne Street. It was a beautiful place.

When I was little, I was very athletic and I would play baseball with my brother Freddie and his friends. He was mean to me because I was the best player.

In elementary school, I was real mean to the boys who were younger than me in my class. I would pull their hair.

My favorite program at home on TV was "Mighty Mouse". My mother used to come right during the time of the program and ask me if I wanted to eat dinner. I would answer, "No, mama!" And then she would tell me that dinner was already on the table.

When I was four or five years old, my mother used to be a horrid cook, and I wouldn't eat the food she cooked. My brother, who ate everything she fixed, would laugh at me all the time (because I got spanked).

When I was little, I used to have beautiful dreams and sometimes nightmares. But I was a lot happier then than I am now because life was simpler then, and I didn't have any problems."

Cynthia (Grade 9 - French I)

SUBPERSONALITIES

PREPARATION:

Discuss the idea that we each have many personalities, often called "subpersonalities", that are active within us, i.e., sometimes our critic, or our judge becomes quite active. At other times our nuturer or our good listener emerges. Each subpersonality represents a manner of acting that is available to us. We all have many personalities available to help us act appropriately in various situations. By learning to recognize these personalities and to understand what they can do for us, we can learn to control them and use them for meaningful purposes. We can also learn how to prevent them from getting us into trouble or from bringing about unhappy results. Here is a list of many commonly perceived subpersonalities:

Judge	Protector (Father)	Warrior
Critic	Child	Slave
Nurturer (Mother)	Intuitive	"Giver"
Counsellor	Saboteur	"Top Dog"
Teacher	Listener	Helper
Lover	"Poor Me" (Underdog)	Sensitive

IMAGERY:

Now travel away to a deep forest where there are many trees...bushes...and plants(pause)...Continue walking through your forest until you come to a clearing where you will see a house or cabin-like structure...This structure contains your subpersonalities(pause)...
Walk up to the front of the house and find a comfortable place to sit...for in a moment you will see your subpersonalities emerge(pause)...Now watch carefully for the door to open...your first subpersonality will

273

appear...Look at it without judgment...Accept whatever you get(pause)...Now a second subpersonality will emerge ...Look at it without judgment...Accept whatever you get (pause)...Now continue doing this until all of your subpersonalities have emerged...Remember to look at them and to accept them without judgment...They are an important part of you(pause)...When all of your sub-personalities have emerged, line them up in front of you ...Ask each one to tell you its name such as, "I am your Judge", "I am your warrior"(pause)...Finish this, then thank your subpersonalities for being with you...and ask them to help you act in a helpful manner toward yourself ...toward others(pause)...When you have done this send them back into the structure(pause)...Now prepare yourself to come back to us here in the room(pause)... On the count of three...

DISCUSSION:

Have your people draw these subpersonalities and write about them. Then ask: "When do your various subpersonalities tend to manifest most strongly?"

"My Judge seems to appear when I meet someone who threatens to compete with me. My Teacher appears when I'm trying to explain something to another person. My Sensitive Person emerges when someone is hurting and needs me to listen to them. I listen sensitively to others."

Sarah (Adult)

VARIATION 1:

When your people have finished the activity and you feel that they have thoroughly grasped the concept of "subpersonalities", you might want to deepen the discussion to include "helpful" and "hindering" aspects of the "subpersonalities". The basic idea is to help your people understand that the personalities are neutral in themselves. It is what we choose to do with them that counts.

L: Think about each of your subpersonalities. Remember that they represent a specific energy in you, an energy that enables you to act in a certain way. But we each have the responsibility to choose how we will act through these subpersonalities. For example, suppose you have a Critic subpersonality. When is your Critic helpful to you? When is your Critic not helpful or perhaps even hurtful?

"My Critic helps me determine what is good for me. When I buy clothes, I'm critical of the various styles and choose only those that look good on me. Sometimes, though, my Critic hurts others when I put them down for doing something that they honestly believe is right. My Sensitve Person helps me pick up vibes from other people, sort of like knowing where someone is without them having to tell me how they're feeling. My Sensitive Person causes me problems when someone criticizes me for doing something they don't like and I take the criticism too personally."

Juanita (Grade 11)

VARIATION 2:

Use this activity for Social Studies lessons by having your people project themselves into a person they are studying (See "Abraham Lincoln" imagery for the basic exercise) and as this person, describe his or her subpersonalities.

EXAMPLE:

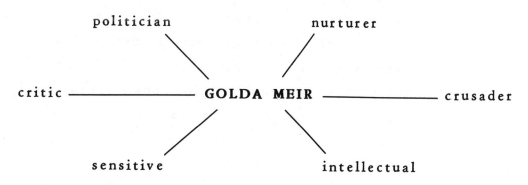

SUCCESSFUL ME

PREPARATION:

Have your people talk about one thing they want to do better or to do well. This might be an academic skill, athletic skill, social skill, body change or the like. Tell them how athletes often use inner visioning to see themselves performing a skill successfully. This is often called "concentration" or "mental preparation". You also might tell them how people are using inner visualization to lose weight, stop smoking, pass tests, stop drinking, and heal disease.

IMAGERY:

Close your eyes and think of one thing you want to do well or better(pause)...Now see yourself doing this thing with great success(pause)...Notice what your body looks like while you are doing this thing successfully...Notice your attitudes about yourself and your abilities...Be aware of your inner feelings ...sensations as you do this thing successfully(pause) ...Feel yourself performing this action...feel it in your whole being(pause)...Notice how others appreciate this talent you have...You have one minute of clocktime equal to all the time you need to image yourself performing this action successfully(pause)...Keep this image firmly in your mind and let it serve as a blueprint for your mind and body to follow(pause)...Always create this mental picture of yourself doing this thing successfully before you actually do it...On the count of three...take a deep breath...exhale...and slowly open your eyes...alert and ready to work with this imagery.

DISCUSSION:

What did you see yourself doing successfully?
Describe how you looked...felt.

VARIATION:

If the entire group is working on a specific skill such as
sinking free throws, giving a concert, presenting a play,
etc., have them visualize this skill and replace general terms
such as "doing this thing" with "sinking free throws", "singing",
"acting" successfully.

TREE OF LIFE

PREPARATION:

Show the students pictures of Trees of Life from various
cultures and have them note the various life symbols
that appear on each tree. Ask the students if they
have ever thought about their own life symbols, objects or
items that mean a lot to them and perhaps even seem to be
sacred or special to them.

IMAGERY:

Today we are going to visit a deep primitive
forest that holds in it many symbols of our
individual lives. This forest existed before
we were born and contains knowledge of who we are.
Take a deep breath...hold it...and exhale with a
slight sigh(pause)...Do this again and as you
you breathe in, imagine yourself taking in
refreshing light...clear air...the fresh smells
of a rainy day...anything that makes you feel
clear and fresh(pause)...Now find a road that leads
to this forest that existed before you were born
and begin walking on this road...Notice the scenery
...Notice if there are other people with you or
if you are alone(pause)...Suddenly you look up
and see a deep rich green forest...and you walk
into this forest...There is plenty of sunlight to
help you see everything in this forest so look
around and note everything you see...smell...
hear...taste...feel(pause)...As you look around
you will see many trees...These are Trees of Life
that belong to various people...Somewhere you
will spot your very own Tree of Life...
You will know that this is your very special

Tree of Life because it will act as if it knows you(pause)..When you have found your Tree of Life, stand in front of it...examine its branches...and notice the various symbols hanging on the branches (pause)...Ask your tree to show you which symbols represent your past(pause)...then ask your Tree to show you which symbols represent the present for you(pause)..Finally, ask your Tree to show you which symbols represent your future(pause)...When you have examined these symbols, thank your Tree for giving you this knowledge...and slowly walk out of your forest...There is plenty of light and you will find it easy to walk back along the same road that you used to enter the forest(pause)...On the count of three...

DISCUSSION:

Suggest that your people draw their Trees of Life and highlight their symbols. Then share these drawings and describe the experience.

NOTE:

You might want to ask the students if they can derive any meaning from these symbols. Be sure to let them know that sometimes we are not able to fully understand the meaning of inner symbolism until days, weeks, months, or even years after we first receive them.

"My past symbols are the two cats in the baskets hanging
from the limbs of my tree. They represent how I used to
be - quiet, not making much ruckus, but silently observing
everything. My symbol of the present are the bees swarming
around the beehives on my tree. This is how my life is
right now - really hectic and lots of activity, and lots
of pressures. I don't like having to live like this, but
I guess it has to be this way. The empty box in the middle
of the tree trunk represents my future. I just don't know
yet what I want to do with my life. As I'm looking at my
tree, though, I see lots of animals on it - the cats, the
bees, monkeys, birds, lambs. I really love animals a lot.
Maybe I'll be a veterinarian."

Jean (Grade 8)

CHAPTER NINE

GUIDED TRANSPERSONAL IMAGERIES

These imageries enable us to explore expanded aspects of human intelligence and consciousness such as the intuitive, mystical, spiritual and cosmic realms of knowing. They include work with energy expressed as feeling, light, color, sound, vibration, symbol and metaphor. They also include the concept of transcendence, or the knowledge that we as humans have the ability to expand beyond ordinary rational, analytical, cause-effect limited ways of thinking about human life and human potential. Transpersonal imageries enable us to examine all aspects of consciousness and learn more about our capabilities.

> There are more things in heaven and on earth than you have imagined...
>
> Shakespeare

The imageries in this section are arranged thematically, and are not necessarily meant to be used in the order in which they appear.

BEFORE YOU BEGIN, PLEASE REMEMBER TO ...

☐ Prepare your people by discussing the importance
of using the particular imagery at this time.

☐ Check to see if they need any movement types of
activities to help settle and center their energy.

☐ Check to see if they need a focusing activity to
sharpen their inner vision.

☐ Make alternate work available in case you have individuals who do not want to do the imagery activity.

☐ Prepare any needed materials such as crayons, paints,
paper ahead of time.

☐ Read the imagery in its entirety and change the
wording and pauses to meet the maturity, readiness,
interest and proficiency levels of your group.

☐ Include a deep breathing/centering exercise to begin
the imagery.

☐ If the imagery does not include a form for ending the
activity (i.e., the "countdown and return to the room"),
be sure you have one ready. You can look at the chapter
on Getting Started for ideas.

☐ Consider adding multi-sensory suggestions such as
"What do you see?...hear?...feel?...smell?...taste?
..." whenever you wish to heighten the sensory experience even if they are not included in the actual text
of the imagery.

BEING OF LIGHT

PREPARATION:

Discuss the meaning and importance of symbolism. Then discuss
the properties of light: how light is often used as a symbol
of higher intelligence, wisdom, spirituality, divinity,
healing, perfection. Use whatever terms are appropriate
to and can be readily understood by your people. You might
want to include stories about wise persons who are depicted
with auras of light around them. You also might want to talk
about how persons who have had near-death experiences
perceive themselves, others on earth, and those who have
passed on as Beings of Light. Light is somehow related to
the very essence of being and is the symbolic expression
of the goodness present in every person, place and thing.

SUGGESTED MUSIC:

<u>Birds of Paradise</u>by Georgia Kelly; <u>Passages</u> by William
Ackerman; <u>Pianoscapes</u> by Michael Jones; <u>Pachelbel
Kanon</u> by James Galway.

IMAGERY:

You are about to embark on a journey where you will
experience your own greatness...goodness...joyfulness
...We will use the symbolism of light to help us have
this experience...Picture yourself on a beautiful
road winding through a lovely countryside...The day
is wonderful, the sun is bright and you can feel its
warmth on your shoulders and face(pause)...Perhaps
there is a slight breeze you can feel dancing gently
on your face(pause)...Ahead of you is a very high

283

mountain...so high that its peaks are hidden in soft white clouds...Soon you will climb to the top and experience a wonderful transformation into light(pause)... Go to the bottom of the mountain and begin climbing to the top...If you need help, look around and find a magic wand, stick, or someone to help you reach the top(pause) ...As you get closer to the top you are surrounded by shiny white clouds and you sense yourself being uplifted by the environment...You sense something wonderful is about to happen(pause)...When you reach the top, look at the sky and notice how brilliant the sun seems to be... brilliant yet friendly...sending you rays of love that fill your whole being(pause)...Suddenly, the sun begins to descend upon you, filling you with a deep sense of peace...joy...calm...well-being(pause)...You begin to feel your entire body...every cell...tissue...muscle... bone filled with this incredible light(pause)...Your head...face...eyes...shoulders...chest...breast...lungs and heart...arms and hands...stomach...hips and thighs legs...knees...feet...Your entire being is filled with this light...Enjoy this experience to its fullest(pause) ...Be aware of your innermost feelings as you experience yourself as a being of pure light(pause)...Now slowly let the sun ascend once again through your body...up through your feet and legs...thighs and hips...stomach and chest... hands and arms...lungs and heart...shoulders...face...eyes ...head...and back again to the sky...leaving you with a wonderful sense of well-being...balance...health... intelligence...wisdom...joy...love(pause)...Let your mind imprint this experience strongly within you...never to be forgotten...a reminder of your greatness...of the greatness of each and every person(pause)...On the count of three, take a deep breath...

DISCUSSION:

Describe your road...the day...the scenery...the mountain.
How did you reach the top of the mountain? By yourself?
With a magic wand or stick? With the help of another?
Have you ever seen yourself as a Being of Light before
this imagery? Seen others this way?

Describe your experiences with the light. Did you have any
bodily sensations? What emotions did you experience? What
images were (and perhaps still are) in your mind? Close
your eyes now and see if you can still remember what it
feels like to be a Being of Light.

What does this experience mean to you? How do others in our
group interpret the experience for themselves? Where (When)
might this imagery be helpful to you if you were to do it
on your own?

SUPPLEMENTARY ACTIVITIES:

Art: Have people draw themselves as Beings of Light. After
drawing their body, they cut out the shape, color it as a body
of light, stuff it with paper or tissue, and hang it as a
mobile.

Movement: Play uplifting music and have people move and dance
out their feelings as Beings of Light.

Drama: Have your people become Beings of Light and observe
their world (i.e., other people, objects, situations, environment) from that perspective. Give them problems to
solve such as "health crises", "economic concerns", "nuclear
power", "politics" and have them work through these problems
as Beings of Light.

BEYOND THIS WORLD

PREPARATION:

Ask your people to talk about their experiences with extra-terrestrial life, with worlds beyond the physical world we experience every day. Some may interpret this as life on other planets, as non-material spiritual worlds, worlds in the mind and the like. Appreciate each person's perceptions in this regard.

SUGGESTED MUSIC:

Starborn Suite; Side Two of Spectrum Suite by Steve Halpern; 2001: Space Odyssey; music from E. T., Star Wars, Close Encounters.

IMAGERY:

We are going to leave this planet and travel outside of the world we know here on earth. Since we will be doing this in our minds, you won't have any problem coming back to this world at the end of your journey. Remember that you are always in command of your imagery experiences. Wherever you go will reflect your personal belief systems about the world so trust your experiences.

Close your eyes and take a slow, deep breath...hold it... and exhale any tiredness, distraction or tension you might be feeling at this time (pause)...(Repeat as needed) ...Surround yourself with a wonderful light that protects you and empowers you to travel beyond this earth(pause) ...Begin your voyage outside of the time and space dimension we know here on earth, and travel away to a world beyond the one we know here on earth...You have one minute of clocktime which is all the time you

286

need to experience this voyage...Remember to examine
everything in the place where you go...the people...
environment...nature...life style...experience these
with each of your senses(pause)...Prepare yourself to
return to us here in the room fully alert and ready to
work with this imagery...On the count of three...

NOTE:

Before asking for a discussion of this experience, you
might give your people colors, crayons and/or markers and have
them draw their feelings. We have found that people are often
more able to retain the fullness of their experience if they
engage in a quiet reflective art type of activity before
talking about it.

DISCUSSION:

How did you surround yourself? What did your light look like?
Describe the part where you traveled to another world.
Describe this "other world". What did you see? Feel? Hear?
   Touch? Taste? Were other people there? If so, how were
   they behaving? What did they look like?
How were you feeling in this world? Were you comfortable?
Is there anything (or are there any times) on earth that
   reminds you of this "other world"?
Would you like to live in this "other world"?
Did your world reflect any advanced or special human char-
   acteristics? Advanced technology?

SUPPLEMENTARY ACTIVITIES:

Art: Have your people draw and/or paint their journey.
Writing: Have them write a composition describing their "other
   world".
Drama: Have them dramatize life in this "other world".

"I found this world highly advanced. People could do things that we only dream about doing today, like sending messages through mind links with others. Telephones weren't necessary because people had perfected ESP communication. There were no wars among nations or gang fights and there was no crime, because people had learned to respect different needs and attitudes. People had perfected the art of synergy where those with differing opinions learned how to merge their minds and give the best of their ideas to the group so that decisions always consisted of everyone's best ideas. Schools were like large libraries and teachers helped kids find and understand information, if the kids needed help. There weren't any hospitals either, but there were special "body shops" where light and energy were used to heal bodies."

Anne (Grade 11)

BODY/MIND CONNECTORS: DIRECTING ENERGY

PREPARATION:

Discuss with your people some of the research pointing to the inseparable connection between mental and physical energy. The body is influenced by the mind and the mind is influenced by the body. Happy feelings cause a relaxed, calm body. And a physically relaxed body causes the mind to become tranquil. Have your people think of times when they relax their bodies to quiet their minds (i.e., jogging, physical exercise, yoga, etc.) and times when they relax their minds to quiet their bodies (i.e., deep breathing, centering, listening to soft music, concentrating on a beautiful object in nature such as a flower, ocean, etc.). Then tell your people that this next imagery exercise will help them better understand their body/mind connection.

NOTE:

Select a few people to do this imagery exercise while the others watch. You need partners, one of whom is large enough or tall enough to lift the other. If this isn't possible, then assign two persons to be the "lifters" for one person. Be careful that everyone is strong enough to do this lifting so that no one will be hurt.

IMAGERY:

(Speaking to those who will be lifted): Stand up now with your partner(s) and allow him/her to lift you off the ground. Don't resist. The idea is for your partner to feel how heavy/light you are(pause). (Once this test has been done, begin the imagery. Send the testers outside the room so they are not influenced by the imagery.)

Those of you being tested, close your eyes...take a deep ...slow breath...and exhale any tiredness or tension you might be feeling at this time(pause)...Now picture the energy field around your body...feel it...visualize it...be aware of its presence(pause)...Now picture all of your energy draining from the top of your head to the bottom of your legs and feet...making you very heavy... so heavy your legs and feet feel like cement bricks (pause)...Your whole body feels like you've gained 100 pounds...You feel yourself becoming so heavy that you are rooted in the ground(pause)...No one could possibly lift you off the ground because you are now too heavy... and as you feel this heaviness...you see your partner trying to lift you off the ground and he/she can't do it... You remain fixed to the ground(pause)...now hold this image in your mind...feel your heaviness...At this time I am going to direct your partner(s) to try and lift you off the ground and as they try...you keep your mind focused on your heaviness...your immovability (Call the testers back in and have them attempt to lift the person. When this is completed have those being tested open their eyes and talk about the experience.)

DISCUSSION:

Could you feel the energy draining to your feet?

What happened when your partner(s) tried to lift you before the imagery? After the imagery?

VARIATION:

Have people imagine their energy going back up and out the top of their head, making them lighter. Then re-do the test.

HAPPY THOUGHTS: PAST, PRESENT, FUTURE

PREPARATION:

Tell your people that in this imagery they will experience happy thoughts from the past, in the present and in the future. You may wish to have them talk about happy memories from the past, thoughts that make them happy in the present, and thoughts about the future that make them feel good before doing the imagery.

IMAGERY:

Close your eyes and take a slow, deep breath...hold it ...now exhale any tiredness, tension or distraction you might be feeling at this time(pause)...(Repeat as needed)...Feel yourself becoming lighter...and lighter ...and lighter(pause)...Slowly, now, as we breathe out ...we remember to use our minds to breathe out any tiredness, tension or distraction...anything that would keep us from feeling totally at one and at peace within ourselves(pause)...Take another deep breath...real deep ...filling all the cells in your lungs and in your entire body with fresh...clear air...hold it...now exhale with a slight sigh...and feel the peace and joy welling up within you(pause)...Now image the sun, very bright, warm... friendly...ready to help you increase your feelings of joy and health...and see yourself stretching your arms up and out toward the sun...drawing the sunlight through the palms of your hands...into your arms... through the top of your head...filling your brain...your face...your neck...your shoulders...relaxing every muscle in the top part of your body(pause)...You can feel this wonderful light streaming through you...Now continue bringing the light down through your breasts...chest... stomach...arms...hands...fingers...thighs...buttocks...

291

legs...knees...ankles...feet...toes...continuing through
you into the earth(pause)...Feel this wonderful light
in your entire body...filling you with a sense of
lightness...brightness...peace...and calm(pause)...
You are a being of pure light...As a being of pure
light...travel away to a wonderful place...a place
of great beauty...where you find a small hill...
Go there to this place with the greatest of ease
(pause)...When you arrive at this place...notice
how peaceful you feel...how beautiful the environment is...how good you feel inside(pause)...
Begin climbing the small hill...and when you reach
the top...find a place to sit down and enjoy the
quiet(pause)...Touch whatever is around you...
Feel things that are there...Smell them...Listen
to the sounds around you...Experience with all of
your senses everything that is there around you
(pause)...Now look into the sky and notice how beautiful the sky is...Enjoy the colors...lights...shapes
...whatever you see there...As you are looking into
the sky...you see something that looks like the inside
of your head...You can actually see your thoughts...
Take a close look, now, and see your thoughts passing
by...These are happy thoughts from the past...
thoughts that once made you very happy and make you
happy today when you think about them(pause)...Now
a new set of thoughts...happy thoughts...enters your
mind...These are happy thoughts from the present...
Notice what these thoughts are like(pause)...Finally...
a third set of thoughts comes floating through your
mind...and these are happy thoughts from the future...
These are the happiest thoughts that could ever be...
Take a close look at these happy future thoughts(pause)
...Now let all of these happy thoughts from the past...
present and future float around and around in your mind
...just like watching a parade(pause)...Notice if

any of the happy thoughts seem more important than others(pause)...Keep these happy thoughts within you... and know that you can remember them anytime you wish... They are yours to have and they will make you feel strong...healthy...confident whenever you call upon them(pause)...Once again become aware of your hill... and the scenery around the hill...and slowly begin to climb down the hill...back to your beautiful place... and back to us here in the room...fully alert...re- freshed...and ready to work with the imagery...Let's take a deep breath...all together...real deep...hold it...feel the power of life surging through you... now exhale with a slight sigh and experience the peace- fulness and calm within you...On the count of three take a slow...deep breath...hold it...exhale...and come back to us here in the room, fully alert...refreshed and ready to work with your experiences...One...two...three...

NOTE:

You may want to have your people draw and/or write about their experience before holding a discussion.

DISCUSSION:

Describe the feeling of the light going through your body.

What were your happiest thoughts from the past? from the present? from the future?

Of all the happy thoughts you experienced, do some seem more important than others?

How did you feel (do you feel) while having these happy thoughts?

SUPPLEMENTARY ACTIVITIES:

Art: Have people draw and/or paint their happy thoughts. You might want to have them cut out their happy thoughts and hang them around the room.

Writing: Have people write creative compositions about their
thoughts.

Drama: Have people choose others to role play their various
happy thoughts and dramatize themselves living with
these happy thoughts.

Energy Exchange: Have your people send each other their
happy thoughts. The receivers sit in front (or in the
center) of the group and receive the happy thoughts
from the senders.

VARIATION:

Have your people focus only on the past, the present or the
future, and bring to mind those things that make them feel
happy.

"I ski well. I walk everyday. I skate on weekends.
I cruise once in a while! I study in school. I listen
in Spanish class. I eat in the cafeteria. I go surfing
in summer. I eat. I chat with my friends."

Theresa (Grade 9 - Spanish I)

"Here is an intelligent girl. Who is it? Me! Cynthia Flores! Ah, yes, the girl who is in the most fantastic French class! Mmm --- I'm fourteen years old. Here is my list of things that will happen in ten years.

I only speak a little French right now - just a little! In ten years I hope I'll speak French very well.

I'll buy a car (a Porsche) for me and I'll be a very rich person. How will you know? Because I will also buy a large house for my mother and family.

I will also buy many dogs because I adore them. Yes, I adore all animals.

Finally, I'll marry a handsome boy who will make a good husband and a nice father. Ah, what a romantic ideal!

I will have one or two children, one boy and one girl. Their names will be Michael and Michelle. I hope that I will be happy."

Cynthia (Grade 9 - French I)

MERGING ENERGIES

PREPARATION:

Prepare your people for this imagery exercise by having them talk about "vibes" or energy fields around people. Examples such as walking in a room where there is lots of tension or sadness, or entering a room where the energy is mellow will help them understand that we always "feel" energies around us. Sometimes we can even feel another's tension or tiredness by standing next to them. Let people tell personal experiences in this regard.

IMAGERY:

Close your eyes...take a slow...deep breath... and exhale any tiredness or tension you might be feeling at this time...Just breathe it out(pause) ...Do this again...taking fresh air in...and exhaling out any tension or tiredness you might be feeling(pause)...Now picture yourself sitting in a circle with everyone here in the room(pause) ...You are aware of a very strong...powerful... loving...helpful energy field around you...Feel this now and see it build in your mind(pause)... Become aware of the energy field of the person on your right...and now the person on your left... Feel their energy field touching yours(pause)... Now direct your energy field to merge with the person on your right...and the person on your left...Continue doing this until you sense one large energy ring around the circle(pause)...Notice how everyone blends, yet you do not loose conscious- ness of your individuality...You are still aware

of being the observer of what you are doing
...It is possible to feel unity with others while
retaining a sense of your uniqueness(pause)...Now
direct your energy to return to you...separating
from the field of your people on the right and left
...and see how this feels(pause)...Which do you
like better...the sense of unity or the feeling of
separateness?...Is it possible to have them
both simultaneously?(pause)...Prepare yourself to
come back to us in the room...refreshed and fully
alert...ready to work with your experiences...One
...two...   Let's talk about this experience.

DISCUSSION:

Did you feel the energy from others? Describe this experience.
What happened when everyone merged energies?
Were you able to feel yourself as the observer?
What changes took place when you withdrew your energy into
you and once again saw and felt yourself (your hands) as
separate from others?

VARIATION:

Repeat the activity while people hold hands. Direct them
to feel their hands merging with those of their neighbor...
feeling their hands losing physical boundaries and becoming one
with others' hands. Then have them once again feel the sense
of separateness...of their hands distinct from others' hands.

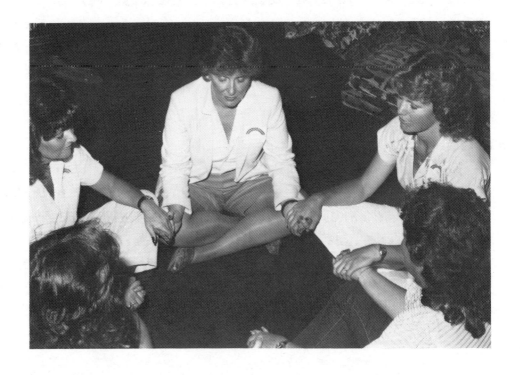

PURPOSE IN LIFE

PREPARATION:

Discuss with people the idea that everyone has a purpose in life, something they've come to do or intend to accomplish. Some people even seem to have many major goals or life purposes. When we know this purpose (or purposes) we can more clearly understand the feelings behind certain key choices we make in life, especially those choices regarding relationships and job/profession.

IMAGERY:

Close your eyes and imagine you are walking in a very beautiful place...a place that has much greenery... clear blue sky...gentle sun...where you feel joy... security...acceptance(pause)...You love being at this place and this place seems to love being with you(pause) ...You have entered this beautiful place because you want to discover your life's purpose and you know that you can find your purpose somewhere here...Continue walking around, thinking about your life's purpose, until you come to a large castle...Stop and look at this castle...examine the color...the shape...the height...the surroundings (pause)...Find a door and enter the castle...Somewhere you will find stairs leading to upper floors(pause)... Climb these stairs until you reach the top floor...and when you do...look around until you find a door marked "Inner Wisdom"(pause)...Enter this room and inside you will find a very wise-looking person who is in charge of great books of knowledge(pause)...Ask this person to show you the great book that has your life's purpose written in it...Be sure to tell the person your name

(pause)...The person hands you the book with the page
open to your story...look now and read it to yourself
...You will find on the page a description of your life's
purpose...things you plan to accomplish in your life
...If you are confused about anything, ask this very
wise person to help you understand the information...
You have one minute of clocktime which is equal to all
the time you need to be with your wise person at this
time(pause)...Thank the person for being here with you...
leave the room...descend the stairs...go out of the castle
...and once again walk through this beautiful place...now
understanding your life's purpose(pause)...Prepare
yourself to return to us here in the classroom...alert...
and ready to work with this experience...On the count of
three...
Take a few moments now to write about your experience.

NOTE:

If any of your people did not meet a wise person or
see the book, assure them that they weren't ready at this time
and that they will receive this information at another time
and, perhaps, even in another manner.

SUPPLEMENTARY ACTIVITIES:

Art: Have your people cut out book patterns and write on the
page what their life purpose seems to be.

Drama: Have them read these pages to each other then act out
in probabilistic fashion, how the individual might
eventually live out this purpose.

"I opened my book and it said, 'David, you are here because you want to learn how to help people by using your hands. That's why your hands always seem so important to you. You like to touch things, feel them, and you love to talk with your hands flapping in front of you. You might use your hands to be a surgeon, a dentist, a chiropractor, a mechanic, a carpenter, or an artist. You have many talents, and you just need to sort out what direction you want to go '."

David (Grade 10)

RECOGNIZING THE LIGHT WITHIN OTHERS

PREPARATION:

When your people are comfortable with and seem to grasp the basic elements of the imagery "Being of Light", lead them in this next imagery designed to help them see this same light in others.

SUGGESTED MUSIC:

Same as for "Being of Light"

IMAGERY:

Repeat the imagery "Being of Light" through the line "Be aware of your innermost feelings as you experience yourself as a being of pure light". Then continue:

Now call to mind your family...friends...other important persons in your life...and see them bathed in this light ...See them as beings of pure light(pause)...How do you feel about them as you are seeing them in this light? (pause)...Now if there is anyone with whom you are in conflict...someone with whom you don't get along right now...someone whom you don't like...or whom you feel doesn't like you...see them bathed in this light(pause) ...How do your feelings toward them change as you see them in the light?(pause)...Now slowly let the image of these people fade away and know that anytime you want to see them as beings of pure light...just like yourself... all you need to do is recall this image(pause)...Let the sun ascend once again through your body...up through your arms...lungs and heart (continue as in "Beings of Light")...On the count of three...

DISCUSSION:

Which persons came into your imagery? Were you able to see each of them as Beings of pure Light? (If some of your people couldn't see certain people in this manner, tell them this is fine, and for some reason, they just weren't ready to see these people as Beings of pure Light. Perhaps another time!)

SEARCHING FOR TRUTH
(Short Form)

PREPARATION:

Ask people to talk about their own perceptions concerning "truth". Is truth objective? Subjective? Is there one truth (the TRUTH, so to speak) that we are all in the process of discovering? Where does "truth" exist?

SUGGESTED MUSIC:

Birds of Paradise by Georgia Kelly; Concertino No. 2 in G Major by Ricciotti.

IMAGERY:

Place yourself on a road in a beautiful place where there are lots of trees and flowers and animals... there might even be a lake, river, ocean or stream nearby(pause)...Walk along your road enjoying the beauty of the day...soaking up the feelings of joy and peace that so often come when we are in nature(pause)... Pay attention to the sounds and smells(pause)...Stop every once in a while and touch things along the way pause)...Continue walking along until you meet someone who will be a guide to you...This guide will help you search for truth(pause)...Ask the guide to show you where you can go to find truth(pause)... Now follow the guide to this place and when you arrive there, look around...What do you see?(pause)...If you are confused or need more information ask your guide to answer any questions you may have(pause)...Prepare yourself now to return to us here in the room(pause) ...On the count of three...

DISCUSSION:

What did your road look like? Trees?...Flowers?...Scenery?...

Were there other people or were you alone?

Describe your guide.

Where did he/she take you?

What was at this place? Describe it.

Did you ask your guide any questions? If so, what?

What did your guide say?

What did you learn about truth?

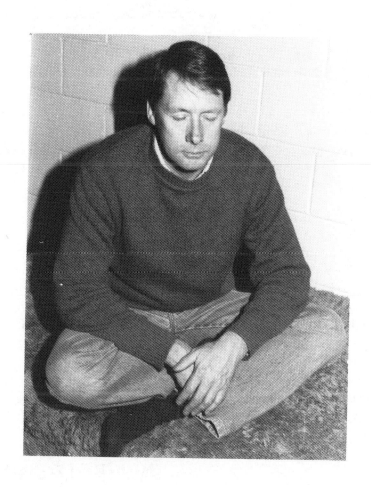

Michelle's class was studying the poem "The Raven" by Poe. The teacher led the students in "Searching for Truth" to help them to discover and learn from their own inner visions and wisdom. In this way, the students have a living experience of Poe's poetic processes as they are presented in the poem.

"In my dream, I saw a high mountain with a castle on top. There was lots of sun shining on the castle, giving it a silverish tone - sort of like magic. I am in a house at the bottom of the mountain. There is a road on my left leading to the castle. "Dream, speak to me!"

'Michelle, right now in your life, you are searching for truth. My sun is the wisdom within you and is always available as your guide. The castle is your inner self which houses all truth. You must go there - inside - whenever you want to know what is right. Remember, you will always have a clear road to get to your castle inside, but you must make an effort to get there. My rainbow is my great reward for you. Don't ever be afraid. Sometimes there will be some clouds getting in your way, but just keep on walking higher to your castle. The clouds will fly away.'

Michelle (Grade 11)

SEARCHING FOR TRUTH
(Long Form)

IMAGERY:

Repeat "Search For Truth" Imagery beginning with...
"Place yourself on a road..."(to) "along the way."
Then continue:

Continue walking along your road until you see
a high mountain appearing before you(pause)...
As you look at the top of the mountain you notice
a wonderful light surrounding the top(pause)...
Walk to the mountain and stop for a moment at the
bottom...It is here that you begin your search
for truth...Start climbing to the top and don't
stop until you reach the top...You can take a magic
walking stick that helps you reach the top if you
think you need this(pause)...Now when you reach
the top you find a palace that is white and gold
(pause)...Enter the door and meet a guide who takes
you where you want to go...Introduce yourself to the
guide and let the guide introduce him or herself to
you(pause)...Tell the guide that you are searching
for truth in your life and you wish to find a room
where you can learn what you need to know in your life
right now(pause)...Your guide takes you to a room
marked TRUTH...Enter this room...See what is there
(pause)...What does the room look like?...Are there
any sounds?...Is anyone else there?...What do you
learn there?(pause)...Do you need to ask your guide
any questions?...Remember to ask your guide to help
you understand anything that doesn't make sense to
you(pause)...Now descend your mountain(pause)...
Walk back down your road...and return here to our room
(pause)...On the count of three...

DISCUSSION:

What did you see along the road?

How high was your mountain?

Did you use a magic walking stick?

Describe the outside of your palace, the inside.

Describe your guide; i,e., name, appearance.

Where did he/she take you?

What was in your room marked TRUTH?

What question did you ask your guide, if any?

What responses did your guide make?

What did you learn from this experience?

SUPPLEMENTARY ACTIVITY:

Art: Have people draw or paint a mural of what they experienced.

Poetry: Have your people write poems about their search for truth.

Writing: Have your people read works of literature whose themes involve a search for truth. Some possible selections would be "Arthurian Legends", "Search for the Holy Grail", "Camelot", and the French poem "Recherche de la Verite". Then direct them to write their own epic.

VARIATION 1:

Repeat the imagery but interchange the words WISDOM, LOVE, INTELLIGENCE, KNOWLEDGE for TRUTH.

VARIATION 2:

Have students in your French class read the poem "La Recherche de la Verite" ("The Search For Truth") and lead a guided imagery similar to the one above, and have them share their experience in French.

"For me the light represents illumination and strength. The high mountain represents the depth of my spirit. At the place where I arrived, I met my spirit. I learned that I am capable of something (of doing certain things quite well), and that I am on the right track. I felt very relaxed during the trip, but I wasn't aware of my body. The feelings that I have from this experience are that my spirit is unlimited in its power."

Jim (Grade 11 -French II)

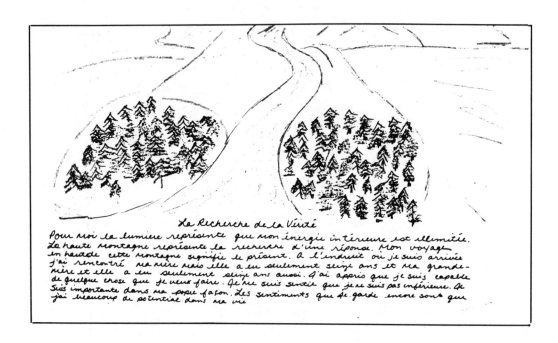

La Recherche de la Vérité

Pour moi la lumière représente que mon énergie intérieure est illimitée. La haute montagne représente la recherche d'une réponse. Mon voyage en haut de cette montagne signifie le présent. À l'endroit où je suis arrivée j'ai rencontré ma mère mais elle a eu seulement seize ans et ma grand-mère et elle a eu seulement seize ans aussi. J'ai appris que je suis capable de quelque chose que je veux faire. Je me suis sentie que je ne suis pas inférieure. Je suis importante dans ma propre façon. Les sentiments que je garde encore sont que j'ai beaucoup de potentiel dans ma vie

"For me the light represents that my inner energy is unlimited. The high mountain represents my search for answers. My voyage to the top of this mountain signifies the present. At the place where I arrived, I met my mother, but she was only sixteen years old. I also met my grandmother, and she was only sixteen. I learned that I am able to do what I want to do. I no longer felt that I was inferior. I am important in my own unique way. The feelings that I still have are that I have much potential yet to develop in my life."

Virginia (Grade 11 -French II)

SENDING AND RECEIVING GOOD FEELINGS: PART ONE
"Developing the Skill"

PREPARATION:

Talk about the importance of good energy, of communicating healthy feelings toward oneself and toward others as well. You might wish to use the example of walking into a room where the vibes are tense and negative in contrast to walking into a room where the feelings are light and happy. We can feel these vibes even if we are not sure what has been happening in the room. The more nurturing the vibes, the better we feel.

IMAGERY:

Picture yourself surrounded by a beautiful golden white light. This is the light of your love, wisdom and joy...Allow your entire being to be filled with this light(pause)...Concentrate on the area around your heart...throat...and forehead...Feel the light very intensely in these areas(pause)...See yourself as a Being of Light...transparent...clear...brilliant ...radiating out to others(pause)...Think of us here in this room and send your light out to everyone here (pause)...Now extend this light to others who are not here...people in your home...in other classes...in other cities...countries(pause)...Check out your body and feelings at this time and see if you are aware of the tremendous energy generated by our group today... (pause)...Remember these feelings and call upon them whenever you feel the need to be energized by good healthy energy(pause)...Prepare yourself to come back to us here in the room...On the count of three...

DISCUSSION:

Have your people discuss the sensations they received while giving and receiving this energy. Some may have experienced heat, warmth, tingling, slight vibrations, buzzing, fullness, whereas others may not have detected anything at this time. Validate each experience as okay!

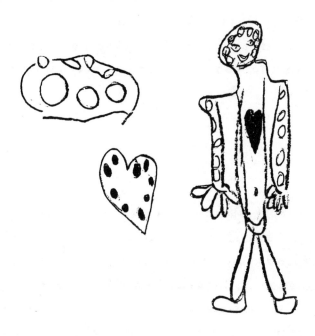

"My heart feels like a watermelon, red and soft, and there are some balls moving inside my heart. The balls are spinning inside my body. They are spinning very fast from my head to my heart and into my arms, and then into Angela and Flor (the people on either side of Eric, holding his hands). The balls are spinning so fast that they are leaving sparks behind like you see from a 'road-runner' car. They make me laugh because they tickle me and make me feel happy."

Eric (Grade 1)

(Eric is very sensitive to energy. He used pink and purple to color his "energy balls".)

312

SENDING AND RECEIVING GOOD FEELINGS: PART TWO
"Asking for Help"

PREPARATION:

Same preparation as for Part One, only this time you invite individuals to stand or sit in the center of the group and receive the energy being sent by the group. Ask who in your group would like to receive good energy at this time. You might also want to specify a certain feeling being sent and received, such as a feeling of "joy", of "wisdom", of "health", of "love", of "confidence" and the like.

IMAGERY:

(Someone has already asked the group to send feelings of confidence to her for a test she will be taking that afternoon. This person is now standing in the center of the group. The leader now leads the entire group in an imagery activity on confidence.)

Picture yourself with a warm brilliant sun about to descend upon you...The sun is friendly and will not burn you. The light from the sun represents your feelings of confidence and these are the feelings we will send to to (name)(pause)...Bring the sun down through the top of your head... filling you with its warmth... and its confidence...You can feel this warmth...this confidence in every cell in your brain(pause)...Now bring the sun down through your forehead...eyes...ears...cheeks...neck ...shoulders...arms...chest...stomach...feeling confidence flowing through every cell in your body, making

313

you stronger and stronger(pause)...Continue bringing this
confidence down through your hips and thighs...legs...
knees...ankles...feet(pause)...Feel confidence flowing
throughout your body...in every cell...making you feel
stronger and stronger(pause)...Now concentrate on (name)
who has asked us to send her/him our feelings of confi-
dence(pause)...Take these feelings that are represented
by the warm sunlight in you and send them to (name) at
this time(pause)...(Name),you quietly receive our feelings at this time...Open yourself to holding within you
our feelings of love and care for you expressed as con-
fidence(pause)...Slowly, now, draw your feelings back
into yourself(pause)...Allow your feelings of confidence
to stay with you and call upon this memory anytime you
need to have confidence in yourself, others, things or
situations. Prepare yourself to come back to us here
in the room, fully alert and ready to work with your
imagery...On the count of three...

DISCUSSION:

Ask the person receiving the feelings to describe the
experience: Did you feel anything while you were
receiving? See anything? Hear anything? Receive
any ideas or insights? What thoughts, if any,
entered your mind while we were sending you confidence?

Have the others respond to the same questions in relation
to themselves sending the feeling of confidence.

NOTE:

We have found that sometimes people experience colors, body
sensations, sounds, voices and unique insights while either
sending or receiving the energy. Whatever is experienced is
always okay! Be sure to tell your people not to be concerned
if they are not always able to understand an experience at the
time they have it. Sometimes full understanding comes much
later.

VARIATION:

Replace the word "confidence" with other feelings related to emotional needs such as love, joy, health, courage.

SUPPLEMENTARY ACTIVITIES:

Art: Have people draw and/or paint themselves filled with the specific energy being sent. They might also paint themselves sending the energy to another. The person receiving the energy paints him/herself receiving the energy from others.

Poetry: Individuals write poems describing their feelings while giving and/or receiving the energy.

EXAMPLE:

Confidence
Rushing at me in purplish reds
Sent by thousands of caring hearts
I shall carry you with me
Wherever I go.

Kellen (Grade 10)

Drama: Review the Imagery "Paint With Love" and have your people paint the individual (and/or each other) with confidence or any other feeling suggested in the variation.

TALKING FROM THE HEART

PREPARATION:

Discuss the following: When you love someone, where do you feel this most intensely? When you feel free and easy, trusting, cared for and appreciated by others, how does your body feel? Illustrate how we are usually open-bodied, upright, facing others with confidence, and not withdrawn, tensed or needing to protect ourselves. We literally open our hearts to others when we love them, feel safe with them, and want to be close.

SUGGESTED MUSIC:

<u>Pachelbel Kanon</u> by James Galway

IMAGERY:

Picture the area around your heart(pause)...Begin to feel lots of energy there...lots of warmth(pause)...Imagine that there is a brilliant field of light energy in front of your heart...Take your hands and feel this field in front of you(pause)...Move your hands in a circular motion and stir up this energy(pause)...Now picture your-self talking to others as they stand in this energy field Everything you say or do is done in and through this energy field of love...And everything everyone else does and says to you is done in and through this energy field of love...What happens when you and others relate from the heart?(pause)...Remember, you can talk to others from your heart anytime you wish by creating this image. Every

316

conversation can be a conversation of love(pause)...Prepare yourself to return to us here in the room(pause)... On the count of three...

DISCUSSION:

What did your brilliant field of light look like? Feel like? What was it like talking with others through this field of light?

Can you still feel this energy around your heart?

SUPPLEMENTARY ACTIVITY:

Art: Have your people draw themselves surrounded by their field of love.

Role Play: Have people work in pairs and practice talking to each other through their field of love.

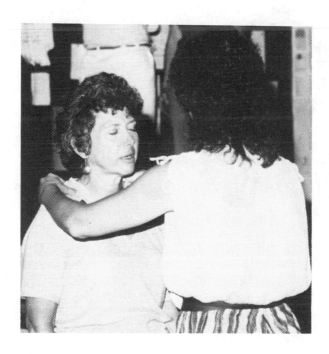

Eric and Angela are brother and sister who were constantly fighting with each other. The counselor working with them led them in several imagery activities similar to "Talking from the Heart." After several sessions, they were able to begin to relate lovingly to each other. These are their comments and drawings in response to the imagery...

"Angela is a nice person because she gives me things. She gives me money. She doesn't tell on me. She waits for me. When she finds something, she gives it to me. Angela has a nice body."
Eric (Grade 1)

"Eric gives me roses. He gives me things and he helps me. I like Eric because he is my brother. I like it when Eric puts a rose in my hair. Eric has pretty eyes. Sometimes Eric is kind."
Angela (Grade 4)

TESTING MIND SIGHT: "Sending and Receiving Colors"

PREPARATION:

Tell your people that they are going to practice their inner visioning skills by sending colors to each other. (Later on you can have them send images of shapes, objects and the like.) Select three or four people to come in front of the group and decide among themselves what color they will send to the others. The small group then concentrates on the color and the others close their eyes, wait to receive a color, then write down what they saw.

IMAGERY:

The people in front of us will select a color that they will send to us in a moment. In order to prepare to receive what color they will send, let's center ourselves with some deep breathing. Take a slow...deep breath... hold it...now exhale any tiredness, tension or distraction you might be feeling at this time(pause)...Let's do this again...Take a slow...deep breath...hold it...now exhale any tiredness, tension or distraction you might be feeling at this time (Repeat as necessary)...Create a blank mental screen in front of you...and wait to receive the color being sent by our small group(pause)... (Direct the small group to concentrate on the color and send it to the whole group.)...Don't think about what the people might be sending...just let your mind be receptive to the color energy...I will give you one minute of clock time which is all the time you need to experience the color(pause)...On the count of three take a slow...deep breath and write down the color you experienced...One...

319

DISCUSSION:

Ask everyone to indicate what color they saw. Then have the small group tell what color they sent. Often we find that the people receiving the color may have seen several colors before seeing the actual one being sent by the small group. Sometimes a member of the small group will mention being momentarily distracted and sending another color besides the one agreed upon by the small group. The more attention you give to the details of the experience, the more exciting are the responses of the group. If some people didn't seem to receive anything, tell them that this inner visioning is a skill like any other skill and needs practicing.

VARIATION:

Replace colors with shapes, objects, countries and the like.

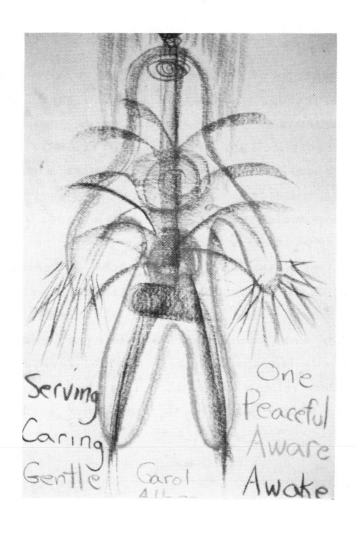

Serving
Caring
Gentle

Carol
Al...

One
Peaceful
Aware
Awake

"I would like to develop my healing talents
through my work with therapeutic touch."
Carol (Adult)

WISE PERSON

PREPARATION:

Discuss the concept of wisdom, what the word means to each
person in your group. You might want to give them terms
such as "conscience", "spirit", "inner voice", and the like.
Discuss how every culture, every civilization seems to have
certain people designated as wise man, wise woman, healer,
shaman, priest, minister, rabbi. These are people who have
the gift of communicating the will of the gods to their
societies or communities. Often, these wise people receive
their information from inner voices, from listening to their
own spirit communicating to them. Ask your people: Do you
ever hear an inner voice telling you what is right? How do
you know when your conscience is talking to you? What are
your ideas about inner wisdom? Do you believe everyone has
an inner wisdom telling them what is right? Give examples
of times when you've listened to your inner wisdom.

SUGGESTED MUSIC:

Same as for "Being of Light"

IMAGERY:

Place yourself in a beautiful forest...filled with
trees, flowers, greenery...a place that is so quiet you
can hear all the natural sounds around you(pause)...
Continue walking through your forest...noticing the
sunlight dancing on the leaves...making patches of light
and shadows on the ground(pause)...As you walk along,
you feel a sense of well-being coming over you...a
feeling of oneness...connectedness with everything

around you...a deep sense of peacefulness(pause)...
Look ahead and you will see a large field with a
mountain appearing through it...In a moment you will
climb this mountain(pause)...Go now to this mountain
and get ready to climb it...If you need help, look
around and find a magic walking stick or anything else
that can help you(pause)...Now begin your ascent...
As you get closer to the top, you notice that in front
of you is a strong field of light...very bright...very
powerful...and this light seems to rest at the top of the
mountain...Continue climbing until you reach the top and
find yourself immersed in this field of light(pause)...
When you reach the top sit quietly and continue looking
into the sky...Soon someone...a very wise person will
come and be with you(pause)...If by chance no one comes
at this time then know you are to be your own wise
person...Look carefully at your Wise Person...Ask him
or her to tell you anything you need to know in your
life right now...anything that can help you live
happily(pause)...If you haven't already done this...
go up to your Wise Person and give him or her some
sign of affection such as a hug...handshake...touch on
the shoulder...kiss...whatever seems appropriate to
both of you(pause)...It's time to return to us here
in the room...so thank your Wise Person for coming to
be with you(pause)...Ask the Person to be available
anytime you need or want him or her(pause)...Turn
around and descend your mountain(pause)...Walk once
again through the field and forest until you find
yourself back with us here in the room...fully
refreshed and ready to work(pause)...On the count of
three...

DISCUSSION:

Describe you trip to the top of the mountain. Did you need help?

What was the light at the top of the mountain like? Was it easy or hard to see in this light? Did you hear sounds or was everything quiet?

Describe your Wise Person. What did he or she look like? Sound like? Act like? Do you know this person in real life?

What did the person say to you? What question(s) did you ask this person? Is there anything in particular you have learned from this experience? Do you have any questions about your experience? Are there more things you'd like to know?

SUPPLEMENTARY ACTIVITIES:

Art: Have your people draw or paint this experience, especially highlighting the dialogue with the Wise Person.

Writing: Each person writes the advice given by their Wise Person on a sheet of paper or index card. These are posted around the room as maxims for everyone to read.

Drama: Have people work as partners. They switch roles. Person #1 assumes the role of the Wise Person for Person #2 and says aloud the advice given #2. Then Person #2 assumes the role of the Wise Person for Person #1 and says aloud the advice given #1.

WORKING OUT CONFLICT

PREPARATION:

Same as for "Talking from the Heart"

SUGGESTED MUSIC:

Pachelbel Kanon by James Galway

IMAGERY:

Picture the area around your heart(pause)...Begin to feel
lots of energy there...lots of warmth(pause)...Imagine
that there is a brilliant field of light energy in front
of your heart...Take your hands and feel this field in
front of you(pause)...Move your hands in a circular
motion and stir up this energy(pause)...Now picture
another person (or other persons) with whom you are in
conflict and have them stand on the other side of your
beautiful energy field...It's as if you are looking at
them through this field(pause)...Now have them enter your
field and talk with you while standing in your field of
love...The two of you are having a conversation...
What happens to the feelings between you as you both
relate in this field of love energy?(pause)...Now take
a deep breath...hold it...exhale with a slight sigh...
and as you do this send out any negative or hurt feelings
that might still be within you and let your radiant
field of love absorb them(pause)...On the count of
three...

DISCUSSION:

How did you feel about this person before talking with them
through your field of love? After talking with them through

your field of love?

SUPPLEMENTARY ACTIVITY:

Art: Have people draw themselves surrounded by an energy field of love. Then add the person with whom they used to be in conflict also surrounded by this energy field of love.

Drama: Have people create a movement activity that represents their feelings while being in this love energy.

Role Play: Have people work in pairs. One person (partner) acts as the alter ego for someone with whom the other person (partner) is in conflict. The first person talks through the field of love to this alter ego with whom he/she is in conflict. Then the alter ego responds. Continue the conversation as long as is needed.

EMBRACING THE POWER OF <u>MIND</u> <u>SIGHT</u>

We are just beginning to explore the vastness of the human mind and the intricacies of its seemingly endless capabilities. Education has always been and continues to be a "leading forth" of human possibility, a gradual revelation of who we are and are coming to be as members of the human community. This unfolding seems to take place best around the fires of our shared stories, stories of incredible human talents, inner visions, insights, discoveries and accomplishments.

Imagery is one of the most powerful tools we have for understanding intelligence and harnessing the seemingly unlimited capabilities of the mind. There was a time when the imaging mind heralded the emergence of human forethought, future visioning and planning, and enabled humans to break free from the bondage of imitative instinctual behavior into the wide open spaces of creative frolic. For it is in the space of unrestricted creative play that the mind continually learns about new ways of being and doing.

Time is now when the imaging mind is foraging roads to heightened human intellectual capacities that we are just beginning to understand. It is only when we honor this imaging mind and give it full reign that we will come to a deeper understanding of what our minds in synergy with our bodies, emotions, spirit and universe can be and do at best.

What we have learned thus far in our work with imagery moves us to promote the continued use of visualization and guided imagery in education (including counseling, therapy, family and social gatherings) and to encourage ongoing research and storytelling of outcomes. Undoubtedly our learnings in this regard will not only reveal to us what imagery can accomplish in education, but perhaps even more important, what inner education, inner teachings and significant new learnings take place when imagery work is used on a regular basis to telescope and amplify the bountiful treasures hidden within us.

> Let's all close our eyes for a brief moment...take a
> slow...deep breath...and exhale any tiredness, tension or
> distractions we might be feeling at this time(pause)

...Visualize with your mind's eye a wonderful world...a world where intelligence, wisdom, understanding, gentleness, unity, peace, and love prevail(pause)...In this world everyone has the ability to fully use what we often think of as super human capabilities...Everyone has these special gifts and is using them well...Everyone is optimally rewarded for having and using these heightened human gifts...Take a full minute to experience this world(pause)...Slowly, now, become aware of the sounds and feelings in this room...and let your consciousness drift back to us here in this space...and as you do this...direct your mind to create an image of you living right now with full use of these heightened human capacities...see yourself and your everyday world thoroughly impacted and influenced by these gifts(pause)...and see others using their gifts for the optimal good of the entire human community(pause)...Keep this image alive in your mind and allow it to remind you of what talents and capabilities are yours for the developing...Prepare yourself to return to us here in this space...refreshed and fully alert...Take a slow...deep breath...exhale...and when you are ready open your eyes...and remember...

With mind sight we can be anything and do anything. We are the orchestrators of energy, the architects of matter. Whatever could be already is within the mind, for the mind knows no limits. The best of what we can imagine is already within us, awaiting our consent to be birthed in the time and space dimension of everyday life. We are the visionaries of promises already fulfilled, for we are both the imager and the image, the seer and the seen, the visionary and the vision. It is with our imaging mind, scanning the skies of inner consciousness, that we come to know the miracle we are.

REFERENCES

CHAPTER ONE: THE IMAGING MIND

Assagioli, R. Psychosynthesis. New York: Viking Press, 1965.

Bogen, J. "The Other Side of the Brain. I, II, III." Bulletin of the Los Angeles Neurological Societies. July, 1969, 34(3).

Bohm, D. Wholeness and the Implicate Order. London: Routledge, 1980.

Brown, B. Stress and the Art of Biofeedback. New York: Harper and Row, 1977.

Brown, B. Supermind. New York: Harper and Row, 1980.

Bugenthal, J. Challenges of Humanistic Psychology. New York: McGraw Hill, 1967.

Capra, F. The Tao of Physics. Berkeley, Ca.: Shambhala, 1975.

DeSoille, R. The Directed Daydream. San Francisco, Ca.: Psychosynthesis Institute, 1965.

Einstein, A. "A Letter to Jacques Hadamard". In B. Ghiseln, (Ed.), The Creative Process: A Symposium. NYC: New American Library, 1952, 45 - 46.

Green, E.E. and Green, A. Beyond Biofeedback. New York:Delacorte, 1977.

Jaffe, D. Healing from Within. New York:Knopf, 1980.

Joy, B. Joy's Way. Los Angeles, Ca.: Tarcher, 1979.

Jung, C. (Ed.) Man and His Symbols. New York: Dell, 1964.

Leuner, H. "Guided Affective Imagery." In the American Journal of

Psychotherapy. 23 (1), 1969, 4-22.

MacLean, P. "A Mind of Three Minds: Educating the Triune Brain". In J. Chall and A. Mirsky (Eds.) _Education and the Brain._ Chicago:University of Chicago Press, 1978.

Maslow, A. _Motivation and Personality._ New York: Harper and Row, 1954.

May, R. _Existential Psychology._ New York: Random House, 1961.

May, R. _The Art of Counselling._ New York: Abingdon Press, 1967.

Moss, R. _The I that is We._ Millbrae, CA.: Celestial Arts, 1981.

Ornstein, R. _The Psychology of Consciousness._ New York: Viking Press, 1972.

Oyle, I. _The Healing Mind._ Millbrae, Ca.: Celestial Arts, 1975.

Pelletier, K. _Toward a Science of Consciousness._ New York: Delta, 1978.

Pelletier, K. _Mind as Healer, Mind as Slayer._ Delaware: Delacorte Press, 1977.

Piccolo, M. and Render, G. "The Relationship Between Mental Imagery and SRA Reading Comprehension in High School Students". Paper presented at the Annual Meeting of the American Educational Research Association, New York City, March, 1982.

Rogers, C. _On Becoming a Person._ Boston: Houghton-Mifflin, 1961.

Rogers, C. _A Way of Being._ Boston: Houghton-Mifflin, 1980.

Schwarz, J. _Voluntary Controls._ New York: Dutton, 1978.

Shorr, J.E. _Psychotherapy through Imagery._ New York: Intercontinental Medical Book Corp., 1974.

Simonton, C. and Simonton, S. Getting Well Again. Los Angeles: Tarcher, 1978.

Singer, J.L. Imagery and Daydream Methods in Psychotherapy and Behavior Modification. New York: Academic Press, 1974.

Sperry, R. "Lateral Specialization of Cerebral Function in the Surgically Separated Hemispheres." In F.J. McGuigan and R.A. Schoonover, (Eds.). The Physiology of Thinking. New York: Academic Press, 1973, 209-229.

Strachey, J. (Ed.). The Standard Edition of the Complete Works of Sigmund Freud. London: Hogarth Press, 1964. (Originally published in 1940).

Sylwester, R., Chall, J. and Wittrock, M. "Educational Implications of Recent Brain Research". Educational Leadership, October, 1981, 6 - 15.

Tart, C. Transpersonal Psychologies. New York: Harper and Row, 1975.

Walsh, R.N. and Vaughan, F. Beyond Ego. Los Angeles, CA.: Tarcher, 1980.

Wilber, K. The Spectrum of Consciousness. Wheaton, Illinois: Quest, 1977.

CHAPTER TWO: BENEFITS FROM USING IMAGERY

Edwards, J. "The Effects of Suggestive-Accelerative Learning and Teaching on Creativity". <u>Journal of the Society for Accelerative Learning and Teaching,</u> 1980, 5(4), 235 - 253.

Elligett, J., Danielson, H., and Holland, M. "A Preliminary Evaluation of the Success Imagery Program in Seven Schools". Report presented at the American Association for the Study of Mental Imagery Conference, Los Angeles, June 25-27, 1982.

Fugitt, E. <u>He Hit Me Back.</u> Rolling Hills, Ca.:Jalmar, 1982.

Galyean, B. <u>Visualization and Guided Imagery in Education: A Preliminary Study.</u> Report for the Center for Integrative Learning, Long Beach, Ca., June, 1982.

Galyean, B. Preliminary data gathered for Part Two of the Research Report completed June, 1982. Part Two to be completed in fall of 1983.

Groff, E. and Render, G. "The Effectiveness of Three Classroom Teaching Methods: Programmed Instruction, Simulation and Guided Imagery". Paper presented at the Annual Meeting of the American Research Association, New York City, March, 1982.

Lange, H. "Increase of Learning Achievement through the Use of Guided Imagery." Unpublished Masters Thesis, Mt. St. Mary's College, Los Angeles, Ca., May, 1982.

Piccolo, M. and Render, G. "The Relationship Between Mental Imagery and SRA Reading Comprehension in High School Students". Paper presented at the Annual Meeting of the American Educational Research Association, New York City, March 1982.

Schuster, D. and Martin, D. "Effects of Biofeedback Induced Tension on Relaxation, Chronic Anxiety, Vocabulary Easiness, Suggestion and Sex of Subject on Learning Rare Words". <u>Journal of the Society for Accelerative Learning and Teaching,</u> 1980, 5(4), 275 - 288.

Shaw, G. "Imagery Use in Creative and High I.Q. Children". Report presented at the American Association for the Study of Mental Imagery Conference, Los Angeles, June 25 - 27, 1982.

Solanto, J. "The Use of Guided Imagery to Enhance Creative Expression in the Classroom". Unpublished paper. November 15, 1981.

Steingart, S. and Glock, M. "Imagery and the Recall of Connected Discourse". Reading Research Quarterly, 1979, 16(1), 66 - 83.

Toomim, M. "Biofeedback and Imagery in the Schools: A Summary of Several Research Projects in Education". Report presented at the Brain/Mind Revolution Conference, Upland, Ca., June 26, 1982.

SUGGESTED READINGS

Bagley, M. and Hess, K. 200 Ways of Using Imagery in the Classroom. New Jersey: New Dimensions of the 80's Publication, 1982.

Benson, H. The Relaxation Response. New York: Avon Books, 1975.

Bry, A. and Blair, M. Visualization for Health and Insight. New York: Harper and Row, 1978.

Bry, A. Visualization: Directing the Movies of Your Mind. New York: Barnes and Noble, 1978.

Canfield, J. and Wells, H. 100 Ways to Enhance Self-Concept in the Classroom: Handbook for Teachers and Parents. New Jersey: Prentice-Hall, 1976.

DeMille, R. Put Your Mother on the Ceiling: Children's Imagination Games. New York: Viking, 1973.

Eberle, R.R. Scamper: Games for Imagination. New York: D.O.K. Publishers, 1971.

Feldenkrais, M. Awareness Through Movement: Health Exercises for Personal Growth. New York: Harper and Row, 1972.

Fiedler, M. Psychophysical Frolic. Pasadena, Ca.: Walden School Publications, 1981.

Fiedler, M. More Psychophysical Frolic. Pasadena, Ca.: Walden School Publications, Pasadena, Ca.: 1981.

Galway, W. The Inner Game of Tennis. New York: Bantam Books, 1975.

Galyean, B. Language from Within. Long Beach, Ca.: KenZel, 1976.

Galyean, B. "The Effects of a Guided Imagery Activity on Various Behaviors of Low Achieving Students" in D. Schuster (Ed.), The Journal of Suggestive-Accelerative Learning and Teaching, 5(2), 1980, 87 - 96.

Galyean, B. "Guided Imagery in Education" in T. Greening (Ed.), Journal of Humanistic Psychology, 21(4), Fall, 1981, 57 - 68.

Galyean, B. "The Use of Guided Imagery in Elementary and Secondary Schools", in J. Singer and K. Pope (Eds.), Imagination, Cognition and Personality, 2(2), 1982-83, 145 - 151.

Galyean, B. "Guided Imagery in the Curriculum" in R. Brandt (Ed.), Educational Leadership, 40(6), March, 1983, 54 - 58.

Gawain, S. Creative Visualization. Berkeley, Ca.: Whatever Publications, 1978.

Gilbert, A. Teaching the Three R's Through Movement, Minneapolis: Burgess Publishing Co., 1977.

Hendricks, G. and Wills, R. The Centering Book: Awareness Activities for Children, Parents, and Teachers, New Jersey: Prentice-Hall, 1975.

Hendricks, G. and Roberts, T.B. The Second Centering: More Awareness Activities for Children, Parents, and Teachers, New Jersey: Prentice-Hall, 1977.

Hendricks, G. The Family Centering Book, New Jersey: Prentice-Hall, 1979.

Hills, C. and Rozman, D. Exploring Inner Space. Boulder Creek, Ca.: University of the Trees Press, 1978.

Houston, J. The Possible Human. Los Angeles: J. P. Tarcher, 1982.

Jacobson, E. <u>Progressive Relaxation</u>. Chicago: University of Chicago Press, 1938.

Jaensch, E. <u>Eidetic Imagery</u>. Trans. by Oscar Oeser. New York: Harcourt, Brace and Co., 1930.

Khatena, J. <u>Educational Psychology of the Gifted</u>. New York: John Wiley and Sons, 1982.

Leonard, G. <u>The Silent Pulse: A Search for the Perfect Rhythm that Exists in Each of Us</u>. New York: E.P. Dutton, 1978.

Lenz, F. <u>Total Relaxation</u>. New York: Bobbs-Merrill, 1980.

Masters, R. and Houston, J. <u>Listening to the Body: The Psychophysical Way to Health and Awareness</u>. New York: Delacorte, 1978.

Masters, R. and Houston, J. <u>Mind Games: The Guide to Inner Space</u>. New York: Dell, 1973.

McKim, R. <u>Experiences in Visual Thinking</u>. Belmont, Ca.: Wadsworth, 1980.

Murdock, M. <u>Spinning Inward</u>. Culver City, Ca.: Peace Press, 1982.

New Games Foundation. <u>New Games Book</u>. New York: Doubleday, 1976.

Oaklander, V. <u>Windows to Our Children</u>. Moab, Utah: Real People Press, 1978.

Parnes, S. et. al. <u>Guide to Creative Action</u>. New York: Scribners, 1977.

Powers, M. and Starrett, R. <u>A Practical Guide to Better Concentration</u>. Hollywood, California: Wilshire Book Co., 1962.

Richardson, A. <u>Mental Imagery</u>. New York: Springer, 1969.

Rogers, C. <u>On Becoming a Person: A Therapist's View of Psychotherapy</u>.

Boston: Houghton-Mifflin, 1967.

Rozman, D. Meditating with Children. Boulder Creek, Ca.: University of the Trees Press, 1975.

Rozman, D. Meditation for Children. Millbrae, Ca.: Celestial Arts, 1976.

Rugg, H. Imagination. New York: Harper and Row, 1963.

Samuels, M. and Samuels, N. Seeing with the Mind's Eye. New York: Random House, 1975.

Stevens, J. Awareness. Moab, Utah: Real People Press, 1971.

Tutko, T. and Tosi, U. Sports Psyching. Los Angeles: J.P. Tarcher, 1976.

NOTE: Many of these books are available through:

THE BOOKSOURCE

6020 Ventura Canyon Avenue

Van Nuys, CA 90401

(213) 994-1760

MUSIC SELECTIONS

Many educators, counselors, therapists, parents and kids working with us have cited the following musical selections as being very helpful to them in their work with imagery. The list is by no means comprehensive and we recommend that you continually look for music that enhances your own imageries.

CLASSICAL

Pachelbel Kanon   Munchinger Stuttgart Orchestra   London Records

Go for Baroque: Greatest Hits of the 1700's   RCA Records

Johann Pachelbel/Johann Fasch   Paillard Chamber Orchestra   Musical Heritage Society, 1991 Broadway, N.Y., N.Y. 10023

An Introduction to the Music of the Baroque Era   Musical Heritage Society.

Pachelbel Kanon (Flute)   James Galway   RCA Records

Great Trumpet Concertos   Maurice Andre   RCA Records

ENVIRONMENTAL

Environments   "Ocean/Lake"; "Wind in Trees/Ultimate Heart Beat"; "Sailboat" Syntonic Research, 175 Fifth Avenue, N.Y., N.Y. 10010

The Sea/The Rain: An Album for Lovers   Ear Records, 7771 Sunset Blvd., Hollywood, Ca. 90046

MOOD AND SOUND

Snowflakes are Dancing, Planets   Tomita   RCA Rocords

<u>Starborn Suite</u>, <u>Spectrum Suite</u>, <u>Comfort Zone</u>, <u>Dawn</u>, <u>Eventide</u>, <u>Whisper on the Wind</u>
Steve Halpern   Halpern Sounds, 620 Taylor Way #14, Belmont, CA., 94002.

<u>Golden Voyage</u>   Vols. 1,2,3,4   Ron Dexter   Awakening Products, 4132 Tuller
Avenue, Culver City, CA., 90230.

<u>Passages</u>   William Ackerman   Windham Hill Records

<u>Callings</u>   Paul Winter   Living Music Foundation, Box 68, Litchfield,
Connecticut 06759.

<u>The Four Seasons</u>   Vivaldi   Angel Records

<u>Gymnosphere: Song of the Rose</u>   Jordan de la Sierra   Unity Records, Box 12,
Corte Madera, CA 94925.

<u>Heaven and Hell</u>   Vangelis   RCA Records

<u>Ignacio</u>   Vangelis   Egg Records/Pema Music Distributions

<u>Inside ll</u>   Paul Horn   EPIC Records

<u>The Moldau</u>   Smetana, George Szell   Columbia Stereo

<u>Music for Zen Meditation and Other Joys</u>   Verve Records

<u>Oxygene</u>   Jean-Michel Jarre   Polydor Records

<u>Reflections</u>, <u>Renaissance of the Celtic Harp</u>   Allen Stivell   Fontana Records

<u>Kalis' Dream: Music for Piano</u>, <u>Pranava: Music for Harp</u>   Alex Jones

<u>Pianoscapes (Michael's Music)</u>   Michael Jones, 28 Carey Rd., Toronto, Ontario,
Canada   M3H 3B3

<u>Birds of Paradise</u>, <u>Sea Peace</u>, <u>Sound of Spirit</u>, <u>Tarashanti</u>   Georgia Kelly

Heru Records   P.O. Box 954 Topanga, CA 90290

Dream Passage, Timeless Motion   Daniel Kobialka   Lisem Enterprises

Piano Solos of Erik Satie   Bill Quist   Windham Hill

You are the Ocean, Rainbow Ray of the Masters   Ruth Schawkie   All Music and Heavenly Music

Mother Earth's Lullaby, Silver Ships   Synchestra   Synchestra Studios

Winter into Spring   George Winston   Windham Hill Records

Superlearning   Tapes to accompany Suggestopedic Methods of Learning, Superlearning Corp., Suite 4D, 17 Park Avenue, N.Y., N.Y. 10016

NOTE: Many of these musical selections may be ordered from:

THE BOOKSOURCE

6020 Ventura Canyon Avenue

Van Nuys, CA 90401

(213) 994-1760

TAPES TO ACCOMPANY <u>MIND SIGHT</u>

The following <u>Mind Sight</u> imageries have been tape recorded by Beverly. They can be used as teaching/counseling aides in classrooms, counseling groups, individual therapy, and homes. They can also be used as individual meditations for personal development.

MINDSIGHT I: <u>Getting Started</u>   (60 min.) $8.50

   Open Eye Exercises: "Mouse"
                       "Home"
                       "Designing Your Own Imagery Journey"
   "Breathing"
   "Centering"
   "Focusing Attention: Color Circles"
   "Favorite Food"
   "Relaxing the Body"
   "Favorite Place"
   "The Rose"

MINDSIGHT II: <u>Guided Cognitive Imageries</u>   (60 min) $8.50

   "Spelling"
   "Ocean"
   "Time"
   "Inner Space of the Body"
   "Discovering Our Roots"
   "Fantastic Machines"
   "Stretching Our Capabilities"
   "Land of Dreams"

MINDSIGHT III: <u>Guided Affective Imageries</u>   (60 min) $8.50

   "Successful Me"
   "Changing Unwanted Feelings"
   "Love"
   "Problem Solving"
   "Happy Memories"
   "Appreciations"
   "Needs and Wants"
   "I Am Unique"

343

MINDSIGHT IV: <u>Guided Transpersonal Imageries</u>   (60 min) $8.50

   "Tree of Life"
   "Being of Light"
   "Wise Person"
   "Talking from the Heart"
   "Working Out Conflict"
   "Purpose in Life"
   "Merging Energies"
   "Searching for Truth" (Long Form)

MINDSIGHT V: <u>Imageries for Young Children</u>   (60 min) $8.50

This tape recording contains adaptations of several <u>Mind Sight</u> imageries for use with younger children. It gives you an idea how to adapt the wording of the imagery scripts to match the interests and readiness level of children whose ages range from approximately 5 - 8 years.

   "Breathing"
   "Centering"
   "Focusing Attention"
   "Floating Free"
   "Fantastic Machine"
   "Successful Me"
   "Paint With Love"
   "Wise Person"
   "Stars"
   "Color of Love"

ORDER FROM: Center for Integrative Learning
                  1442-A Walnut St., Ste. 317
                  Berkeley, CA 94709

   MAILING COSTS: $1.00 for first tape. Add $.25 for each additional tape. California residents add 6.5% sales tax. All prices quoted are in U.S. funds and are subject to change without notice. <u>Orders must be prepaid.</u>

EXPANDING HUMAN INTELLIGENCE: A Six Tape Series
   Tape 1: An Overview of Brain/Mind/Consciousness Research
               (Beverly Galyean, Ph.D.)
      Optimum performance in learning, widening vision of genius,
      role of neural circuitry in learning, Sheldrake's theory
   Tape 2: Implications of the Brain/Mind Revolution for Learning
               (Diane Battung, Ph.D.)
      Explores 42 potential developments that might foster expanded
      learning capabilities
   Tape 3: Introduction to Guided Imagery (Galyean)
      Presents the six basic steps for using guided imagery activities.
      Helpful for both people new to visualization processes, and those
      experienced in guided imagery.
   Tape 4: Body/Brain Connection (Maureen Murdock, M.A., M.F.C.C)
      The body as a Memory and Learning system, holographic brain
      theory, multimodal learning
   Tape 5: Learning Modalities (Murdock)
      Mindmapping, optimal learning environments, learning preferences,
      brain dominance, NLP, triune brain theory
   Tape 6: Accessing the Fullness of our Human Potential (Battung)
      Multimodal processing, techniques for belief system fluidity,
      mind-body link, dreams as part of the meta-language, body wisdom.

   This full series of six 90 minute tapes comes in an album.
            Cost: $49.95 plus $4 shipping

THE INTUITIVE MIND: A Three Tape Series ... Beverly Galyean, Ph.D.

   We can train ourselves in the skills that make us more able to
   access intuitive insights, and can learn how to be open to
   intuition all the time. Central to this process is the ability
   to fantasize. Dr. Galyean skillfully combines the theory and
   practice of developing intuition in this public lecture.
   (3 cassette album: $24.95 plus $3 shipping)

IMAGES, FEELING TONES AND METAPHORS: LEAPING BEYOND PIAGET
   A Three Tape Series ... Beverly Galyean, Ph.D.

   Piaget's four ways of knowing (sensory-motor, preoperational,
   symbolic and logical) are no longer sufficient to encompass
   our expanded levels of consciousness. In this public lecture
   Dr. Galyean explains how brain/mind/consciousness research
   both supports and helps us access unlimited knowing. The
   work of Paul MacLean (Triune Brain Theory) and David Bohm
   (Theory of Enfolded Reality) as well as the concept of the
   holographic brain are explored in detail.
   (3 cassette album: $24.95 plus $3 shipping)

ORDER FROM:
   Center for Integrative Learning   Prices are U.S. funds and are subject
   1442-A Walnut Street, Suite 317   to change without notice. California
   Berkeley, CA 94709   residents, add 6.5% sales tax.
   Attn: Anne Bruetsch, J.D., Director   Orders must be prepaid.